COIN HU[.....]
.....IN DEPTH!

by Dick Stout

Published by
White's Electronics, Inc.
Sweet Home, Oregon

Editor: Mary Hand

DEDICATION

Once again I dedicate this,
my second book, to my wife Fay.....
She has always understood my ways, my wanderings and my
dreams, no matter how far fetched....
She is far more valuable than any treasures I shall ever
hope to find in my lifetime...

ACKNOWLEDGEMENTS

White's Electronics for their consistent dedication to quality products and the preservation of the treasure hunting pastime.

Mary Hand, for her knowledge and expertise in putting this text together.....

All of the many detectorists I've met over the years. I consider you my close friends, and hope you continue to find those treasures that make life worthwhile....

Photos by Fay Stout

FOREWARD

Quite apart from his considerable expertise with a metal detector, Dick Stout is one of the pastime's great communicators. His passion and willingness to lock horns with over-zealous legislators; his fight for the rights of the individual to pursue the pastime unhindered by bureaucracy, has become the stuff of treasure hunting's folklore. This, Dick Stout's latest book, is yet another facet of the man's character - a willingness to share his years of accumulated knowledge with others.

Over the past decade I have enjoyed immensely, the privilege of treasure hunting in his company, both in England, hunting for Roman coins in the Cotswold Hills, to coinshooting the United States' Eastern Seaboard beaches. Read and mark his words well, whether you are new to the hobby or a seasoned veteran, you will learn from this man.

Above all else though, Dick Stout is a treasure hunter's treasure hunter. In these times of the Politically Correct, I make no apology for making use of an old English adage of personal recommendation, that, *Dick Stout is the kind of guy it's a pleasure to have a beer with.*

John Howland/Didcot, Oxon, England

(John Howland is the author of *"Treasure From British Waters"*, former Special Projects Coordinator for the National Council for Metal Detecting in the UK, and author of well over 100 treasure hunting essays and articles).

TABLE OF CONTENTS

PREFACE

Finding coins with a metal detector does not take a great
deal of skill.....finding old and valuable coins does! It also takes
desire, patience and perserverance! If you own a metal detector or
are considering purchasing one, and you want to increase your
odds of finding these coins, then this book was written for you.
For a little over twenty three years I've searched here and abroad,
using every brand and model of metal detector imaginable. No, I
am not a millionaire, nor am I on "easy street". I am however
financially better off because of my efforts, and grateful that I
found a pastime that is not only enjoyable but profitable as well.

The successes I've had coinhunting were often the result of
common sense, always the result of thorough research, and sometimes the result of trial and error. As a result I am confident that if
you read and utilize the information that follows you too will have
similiar success, and your coin collection will not only grow in
numbers but increase in value as well. Old and very valuable coins
are waiting to be found.....finding them however is up to you!
In the pages that follow your reaction to some of my theories or
recommendations might be.... "of course, I know that", or....."why
that's only common sense!" What I will ask however is that you
consider what I have to say, give my theories and recommendations a try and then analyze the results. I am confident that if you
do this you will have success, find renewed enthusiasm and most
importantly develop the attitude that you can find any treasure
you seek.

There are many metal detecting books that promise
treasure, riches, and almost always imply that you will become
wealthy! The bottom line...they offer little of substance, are
usually written by ghost writers (someone representing the listed
author), and typically leave you no better off than when you
started reading. This book differs in that respect, offering only

tips, ideas and methods I've learned through years of practical, in the field experience. I'll share all my techniques and theories that will help you find the older coins you seek, and by doing so hopefully give you an advantage over the competition.

I will frequently refer to "those deeper, more valuable coins" because that is what we're after, and they are in a class by themselves. Barber, Liberty Seated, Indian Heads, Large Cents and Bust coins are what we seek, and such coins are almost always found at depths of six to twelve inches ..... an area that has never been addressed in previous books. Not so within these pages.

Let's also get one nagging theory and question out of the way. Yes, I do believe that coins sink deeper year after year, but it's a moot point! It's a subject that need not be addressed or debated because frankly we will never know! The reality is that older coins are almost always deep, and gaining that inch or two more in depth is important. That extra inch, that extra advantage has been my objective for the past 22 years, and it should be yours as well. Your detector is state of the art, quite capable of going deep, but setting it's controls to the max, and taking it to the right places is what will make you the better coinshooter!

Last but not least....I've met hundreds of detectorists over the years, and many have told me that they know their detectors inside out. They talk about coils, controls, conductivity, caches, electromagnetic fields, eddy currents, elliptical coils, Faraday shielding, frequencies and false signals. They discuss filters, discrimination, Ni-Cad, Ferrous, Non Ferrous, Ten Turn Controls, Zero Discrimination and anything else that might impress. The bottom line.....none of this matters if you are not searching the right area! Technical knowledge is certainly important, but knowing how to research is first and foremost if you are to succeed. *You cannot and will not find coins where they don't exist!* Metal detectors are not atom smashers....they are very easy to use, and quite capable of finding treasure, but only if you take them to the right places.

If you are intrigued by the possibility of finding old and valuable coins, and if you are ready to work hard, get dirty and have fun at the same time, let's get started.....

Rowlett, Texas   D.S.
November 1994

COIN HUNTING .....IN DEPTH!

by Dick Stout

THE LURE OF COINS

People have been collecting coins for hundreds of years, making numismatics one of the oldest hobbies in the world. Coins not only have collectable value....they are "spendable" ..... redeemable for goods, and I can't think of any other pastime that offers this distinction. If you have used a metal detector for any period of time you already know something about numismatics. Likewise if you are a beginning coinshooter, you will quickly become knowledgeable without trying. Your desire to learn more about your finds, especially their worth, will draw you deeper and deeper into the numismatic field!

Each and every coin found with your metal detector is one more than you started with, and many will offer additional rewards because of their age, scarcity and demand. If you have the ambition, the determination and are willing to research and work hard you can find these valuable coins fairly consistently.

I began coin hunting with a metal detector early in 1970 after I became somewhat interested in numismatics. I was reading a weekly numismatic newspaper and noticed a classified ad for metal detectors..... it said....in so many words, "find those rare dates you've been looking for without spending a cent"! I studied that ad, and I remember thinking .... if I spend $200 on one of these contraptions can I really find the coins I need for my collection? Being a "doubting Thomas", I was extremely skeptical, but interested nonetheless. I sent for information, visited a local dealer, and the rest is history. (I know what you're wondering.... no I haven't found "all" the coins I was looking for, but I found a pastime that I enjoy, that is intriguing and that provides me with a profit, and I have no doubt of course that eventually I will find all those coins I seek)!

"THEY TELL US THAT MONEY DOESN'T BUY HAPPINESS BUT WOULDN'T IT BE NICE TO FIND THAT OUT FOR OURSELVES"

LEARNING ABOUT COINS

If you are a newcomer to the coinhunting pastime, not familiar with numismatics, and you have just purchased a metal detector you should begin your learning process immediately. Learning what your finds are worth is important, easy to do, and to start this process you should purchase R.S. Yeoman's "Guide Book of United States Coins". It's published annually by Western Publishing in Racine, Wisconsin, is available at any bookstore, and is referred to as the "Red Book". The Red Book offers visual identification of every United States coin, descriptive guidelines for grading, the market value for each grade, and at $8.95 it's a bargain!

The coin prices in the Red Book are *retail*, or what you might expect to pay for a coin if you were to purchase it from a coin dealer. Western Publishing also publishes the "Blue Book" and the prices therein are wholesale, or what a dealer would pay you for the coin. You should have both in your possession to get a feel for what any coin is worth. The ultimate payback or reimbursement is up to you and your ability to negotiate.

I would also recommend you find the latest edition of James F. Ruddy's *Photograde.* This book was once considered the bible for grading coins, but has since been replaced by a more complicated numerical system, which I personally find very confusing and somewhat unreliable since it all depends on the eye of the beholder. Photograde will continue to be my favorite reference book for grading, and I can tell you that its the same for many other collectors as well. It's loaded with clear, definitive pictures.....not a lot of numbers, and in my mind leaves little doubt as to how to grade a coin.

Older US coinage not only offers intrinsic value and monetary return, but aesthetic beauty that today's coinage cannot begin to match. These older coins are detailed, ornate and classic works of art. For example there's no comparison between the buffalo nickel and today's Jefferson five cent piece, nor can the Roosevelt dime match the beauty of the winged Mercury. My personal favorites....The Buffalo Nickel and the Walking Liberty Half Dollar! Two classic patterns!

The Walking Liberty Half Dollar and the Buffalo Nickel.

EARLY COINAGE

Become familiar with all early coin denominations; they are not nearly the same as those you are familiar with today. When the U.S. Mint was established in 1792, and for more than half a century since, there were no paper notes. Money was coinage.....plain and simple! Coins were in denominations from half cents going all the way up to $10. It should also be noted that the $10 coin equaled the $100 note of today in buying power!

> *"Because paper money did not exist, the early colonist carried a lot of coins and a lot of weight. If he had $1.00 on his person he would have had 1 1/2 pounds of coins to carry around. Why is this important? Simply to make a statement about how many coins had to be carried, and how many just may have been lost!"*

Another interesting sidelight ......paper money, when it did come along, was not accepted as readily as the coin. A number of states issued paper notes, as did local banks. Many of these banks went out of business, and counterfeiting became popular. Paper money was considered too new and too risky..... coins were not! Even if the government failed, a coin containing 1/2 ounce of silver would still be worth 1/2 ounce of silver! That is also why tokens became readily accepted....it didn't matter who was backing them; as long as you were getting a penny's worth of copper it mattered little whether it was a coin or a token.

There were more coin denominations in early times, and for good reason. Things were quite different then. There were low prices, a more leisurely pace, and yes a half cent could actually buy something! Half cents, and two and three cent pieces were common. Today we are down to six denominations...a cent, nickel, dime, quarter, half and of course the Susan B. Anthony dollar, which for all practical purposes is not circulated.

WHAT MAKES A COIN VALUABLE

The first factor that makes a coin valuable or rare is mintage! Mintage of course means the number of coins struck for any particular date. The fewer coins minted....the fewer there are to collect, and as would be expected the fewer there are in the better grades. Demand also is also important. If a dealer has two coins of equal mintage, and one is more "popular", it's price will be higher than that of the other piece. The logic of course is you can't ask a lot of money for something few people want! Last but not least the physical condition of the coin is also a consideration. Those coins showing little or no wear are always worth more!

"ANYBODY WHO THINKS THERE'S A SHORTAGE OF COINS HASN'T BEEN TO CHURCH LATELY!"

KEYS & SEMI-KEYS

As you continue to learn about numismatics you will become familiar with the "key coins" in each series. These are the dates or years that are rare, that offer the greatest monetary return, and are reason for celebration when you recover one. Examples.....the 1877 Indian Head Penny, the 1909SVDB Lincoln Cent, the 1937D three Legged Buffalo Nickel and the 1916D Mercury Dime.

You should also become familiar with the semi-key's as well. These are coins that do not necessarily have extremely low mintage figures but are valuable because they are scarce in the better grades. One such example.....the 1914S Lincoln Penny. It has a mintage of 4,137,000 but it's value in extra fine condition is $31.00....not a bad return for a penny! Always check all of your coin finds before throwing them in the proverbial cigar box or junk jar. You might be surprised.....

A FEW TO LOOK FOR

INDIAN HEAD CENTS
KEY DATES: 1864L, 1869 over 9, 1877, 1888 over 7, 1908S
and 1909S.
SEMI-KEY DATES: 1866, 1867, 1868, 1869, 1870, 1871,
1872 and 1876.

LINCOLN CENTS
KEY DATES: 1909SVDB, 1914D, 1922 Plain, 1931S, 1955
Doubled Die and 1972 Doubled Die.
SEMI-KEY DATES: 1909S, 1911S and 1914S.
BARBER NICKELS
KEY DATES: 1885 AND 1886
SEMI-KEY DATES: 1890 and 1912S

BUFFALO NICKELS
KEY DATES: 1913D (VARIETY 2), 1913S (VARIETY 2),
1916D Doubled Die, 1918D(8 over 7), 1937D Three Legged.
SEMI-KEY DATES: 1914D, 1915S, 1921S and 1926S.

JEFFERSON NICKELS
KEY DATES: 1943P (3 over 2) and 1949D (D over S).
SEMI-KEY DATES: 1939D, 1950D and 1955D (D over S).

BARBER DIMES
KEY DATES: 1895, 1895O, 1896O, 1896S, 1897O and
1901S.
SEMI-KEY DATES: 1892S, 1893O, 1894O, 1895S, 1903S,
1904S and 1913S.

MERCURY DIMES
KEY DATES: 1916D, 1921, 1921D, 1942(2 over 1) and 1942D(2 over 1).
SEMI-KEY DATES: 1926S AND 1931D.

ROOSEVELT DIMES
KEY DATES: None in particular
SEMI-KEY DATES: In better grades....1949, 1949S, 1950S and 1951S.

BARBER QUARTERS
KEY DATES: 1896S, 1901S and 1913S.
SEMI-KEY DATES: 1892S, 1897O, 1897S, 1901O, 1901O and 1913.

STANDING LIBERTY QUARTERS
KEY DATES: 1916, and 1923S.
SEMI-KEY DATES: All up to 1925....relief and detail are most important.

WASHINGTON QUARTERS
KEY DATES: 1932D, 1932S and 1943S (Doubled die obverse).
SEMI-KEY DATES: 1936D, 1937S, 1938 and 1939S.

BARBER HALF DOLLARS
KEY DATES: 1892O, 1892S, 1893S and 1897S.
SEMI-KEY DATES: 1892, 1893, 1896S,1897O, and many others in this series....fine condition and above....!!

WALKING LIBERTY HALF DOLLARS
KEY DATES: 1916S, 1921, 1921D and 1938D.
SEMI-KEY DATES: 1916, 1916D, 1921S and others in the better grades.

"WE SPEND OUR LIVES TRYING TO ACCUMULATE MONEY, THEN LOOK BACK TO THE TIMES WHEN WE HAD NONE AND CALL THEM THE "GOOD OLE DAYS!"

QUALITY VS. QUANTITY

As I stated earlier....anyone with a metal detector can find coins, but not everyone with a metal detector can find "old" coins. Newer, clad coins are everywhere, but as a professional coin hunter your goal should be finding those that offer the greatest return on your time. New coins should always be considered incidental and accidental. Save them until you have enough to purchase one or two coins with numismatic value and investment potential.....a key, semi-key or gold coin that will appreciate over the months and years to come.

"There are many detectorists who will keep everything they find simply to have something that is impressive to look at, and yes, thousands of coins in a box look impressive, but how much do they have in actual dollars and cents?"

There are many detectorists who will keep everything they find simply to have something that is impreessive to look at, and yes thousands of coins in a box look impressive, but how much do they have in actual dollars and cents? Probably not a whole lot, and they'll be six feet under before it is worth anything (wheaties as well!).

As you coin hunt never assume that what you find is not

worthy of further evaluation. Until you become intimately familiar with US coinage check each and every one of your finds in the Red Book. Approximate the condition based on the descriptions in the book and arrive at a value. Likewise if you find an old pen knife, a toy soldier, a spoon or button, learn more about them before storing them away or disposing of them. You just might be overlooking the best find of all!

Save your routine finds, and invest in a gold coin or key coin that will increase in value as the years go on.

"A DIME IS A DOLLAR
WITH ALL THE VARIOUS TAXES DEDUCTED!"

COIN CONDITION

Always keep in mind that the condition of any coin you find is important when it comes to it's monetary value or return. Even relatively common date coins will be more valuable if in the higher grades. As an example an 1886 Indian Head Cent is worth only $2.25 in Good Condition, but in Extra Fine Condtion it's valued at $40.00. Also an 1895O Barber quarter in Extra Fine

Condition is worth $75.00, but if it's marred, worn and graded in Good condition it's value is only $4.00.

What this means of course is that you must always be careful when you dig old coins. Hasty, careless recovery can be extremely costly. You are, in a manner of speaking, in the rare coin business, and this means that any coin you find is potentially a rare one....it's value is based on it's scarcity and it's overall condition. One little nick or scratch from a trowel or knife can mean a loss of money. Always recover any target or coin carefully, keeping in mind that it just might be that one find that puts you on easy street!

KEEP RECORDS

If you are to be a successful coin hunter <u>document</u> all of your finds and in-the-field experiences. Record each and every outing with your metal detector so that you can analyze the results and reflect later on. Hindsight, as we all know, answers a great many questions, and keeping detailed records will surely answer a few for you. As you continue your searching this information can prove useful such as when you want to concentrate on finding a specific key coin, or when you only have a limited time to search.

How you keep or record this information is up to you. You can log it in a notebook or on index cards, or you might keep it in your computer. Whatever method you decide on keep track of dates, sites, ground and weather conditions, coin finds (by date), non-coin finds, and the various hot spots within the site itself. Record as well the detector(s) you used, the size of the coil(s), and any noteworthy control settings. Document the length of time you spent at the site, and any thoughts you may have concerning the viability of future searches.

I review my recorded data frequently, and often come up with new ideas or thoughts on how I might improve my odds at various sites. One such example.......an old carnival ground in New Jersey produced many early 1900 coins, and after searching it over 20 times I felt fairly certain it had little more to offer. Then a year and a half later I began looking through my records, and noticed that at this particular site I'd found quite a few old coins along the edge of a wooded area. At the time I searched the site I hadn't given this any further consideration, but I began to wonder if perhaps the wooded area <u>itself</u> would give up a few good finds. A return visit, and a thorough search did provide quite a few old coins, and a lot of insight into how I had to review my previous coinhunting ventures.

I cannot be sure why this outer area gave up additional coins. I can only assume that the carnival site was somewhat larger years ago, and that the vegetation crept in over the ensuing years, camouflaging what had been prime ground before.

You will continually learn a great deal by keeping good records. Knowing the dates a site was in use will give some perspective of what you can expect to find. On the other hand if this information is not known, the dates of your finds will tell you. Your record keeping will also indicate that some sites are more productive at different times of the year, perhaps just after a good rain. Start this documentation now, and you will quickly learn why it's important!

Another interesting sidelight to <u>my</u> record keeping was the increase in older coins as I continued to coinhunt. Each month, each year the percentage increased, as did the overall value of my finds....a direct reflection of my in-the-field experience, and exacting research. The figures that follow are an example ...

	1975	**1980**
INDIAN HEAD CENTS	.17%	1.25%
WHEAT CENTS	19.08%	20.02%
MEMORIAL CENTS	53.41%	48.21%
BARBER NICKELS	.05%	.85%
BUFFALO NICKELS	.84%	.90%
JEFFERSON SILVER NICKELS	.90%	1.87%
JEFFERSON CLAD NICKELS	10.19%	9.01%
LIBERTY STANDING DIMES	.05%	.75%
BARBER DIMES	.90%	1.89%
MERCURY DIMES	1.75%	2.95%

STORAGE

When you are in the field detecting be sure to separate your better coins as you recover them. If you have an apron put them in the "keeper" section, and if you have reason to believe they might be even more valuable, wrap them in a piece of tissue paper, and put them in your pocket. A coin's value can diminish quickly with one scratch or mark. Better safe than sorry!

After returning home, store these better finds so they are safe from "accidental" damage. For short term storage (1 to 6 months) I like the 2x2 cardboard holders. They are inexpensive and can be purchased at most any coin or hobby shop. Label each 2x2 with the date you found the coin, the site and the approximate condition or grade. If you find an "exceptional" coin, (one that is worth a great deal of money) place it in a 2x2 and place it in a safe deposit box or in a safe at home.

As you continue coinhunting and become more familiar with numismatics, you will soon learn that how you store or keep your coins is extremely important. In the beginning we tend to worry more about security than we do about preservation. We worry about being burglarized, about our children taking coins for candy or ice cream, and never consider that "how" we store our coins should be of greater concern. Later on, perhaps a year or two down the road, we suddenly become aware that our prized collection is becoming marred with dullness, fingerprints and other mysterious spots....the result of earlier ignorance and containers or holders not suited for long term storage.

> "In the beginning we tend to worry more about security than we do about preservation. We worry about being burglarized, about our children taking coins for candy or ice cream, and never consider that "how" we store our coins should be of greater concern."

You will find the 2x2 cardboard holders I mentioned above, and 2x2 clear vinyl flips available at area coin shops, but they are meant for short term storage only. Most of these holders contain PVC (polyvinylchloride), a chemical found in many plastics, and one that over time will breakdown and eventually damage your coins (holders made of Mylar are somewhat better, but should also be considered for short term storage only).

For long term storage keep your coins in tubes made of "inert" plastic. They are usually translucent or cloudy in appearance, and offer safe, long term storage. Your main concern in using these tubes is the scratching of coins when dropping them in. Be gentle, avoid constant handling and "upside/down" movements of the tubes themselves.

Finally hard plastic holders (2x2's) are for the "special" items in your collection.....those that will appreciate in value over time. Here again there are many types available....some come in pieces that can be screwed together.....most are air-tight and water-tight. They are more expensive, but do provide safe, long term storage, and are certainly worth the investment.

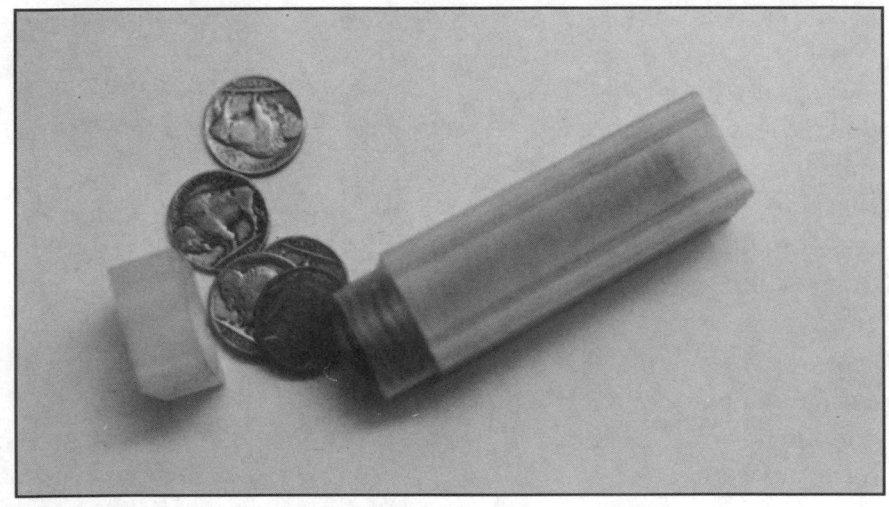

Coin tubes made of inert plastic will serve you well for long term storage of your older finds.

Whatever method of storage you choose be sure the seller guarantees the product is safe for coins. Many older holders and books containing damaging chemicals can still be found in stores, at flea markets and garage sales. If you are the least bit in doubt, do not buy!!

Make it a point to check your coins at least once or twice a year. Watch for dulling, spots or mildew, and inspect the coin holders themselves for hints of damage or breakdown. Improper storage, and careless handling can cause you a large financial loss should you ever decide to sell a coin or a collection.

On another note....if you decide to keep your collection at home be sure your homeowners insurance policy will cover it! If not, and if you cannot afford an additional premium, invest in a fireproof safe (or rent a safe deposit box at your bank). I don't have to tell you that home burglaries today are increasing. Treat your coins like one of the family. Keep them in an area that is reasonably stable and constant in temperature and humidity. Never store them in the attic or basement (no matter how great you think your hiding place is). Attics get hot, and basements get wet. Both heat and humidity, working along with PVC will quickly turn that good coin into a bad one! It's also not a bad idea to throw a few small bags of silica gel into your boxed collection to ward off humidity.

"MONEY MAY NOT MAKE A PERSON HAPPY BUT IT KEEPS HIS CREDITORS IN A BETTER FRAME OF MIND!"

HANDLING COINS

Handle any potentially valuable coin by it's edge, and never put your fingers on the surface of the coin. Likewise when showing a coin be sure it's held over a surface that will not scratch or mar it should it be dropped!

Cleaning a coin is tempting, but it could very well decrease it's value. The wear and tear of a coin over the years is part of it's natural beauty, and serious coin collectors never, ever attempt to clean a valuable coin. If you have such a coin merely rinse off the surface dirt with warm water, and let it dry on it's own Then put it in a protective holder, and store it in a safe, protective place (away from heaters, sunlight, and any other potentially damaging outside influence).

" MOST OF US HAVE ENOUGH MONEY TO PAY OUR TAXES . . . . WHAT WE NEED IS SOMETHIN TO LIVE ON!!"

Always handle a potentially valuable coin by its edges . . . .

DIRECTORY
COIN SUPPLY COMPANIES

BROOKLYN GALLERY COINS & STAMPS, INC.
8725 4th Avenue
Post Office Box 090-146
Brooklyn, New York 11209
Telephone: 718-745-5701
Fax: 718-745-2775
Handles anything and everything connected with
numismatics....great 75 page catalog for only $2.00.

CAPITAL COLLECTORS PLASTICS COMPANY
628 North Erie Street
Post Office Box 543
Massillon, Ohio 44648
Telephone: 216-832-4287
Fax: 216-832-4416
Carries full line of coin holders

BEST SUPPLY COMPANY
Post Office Box 18095
Indianappolis, Indiana 46218
Offers books, holders and accessories for the collector

CHIEF COIN SUPPLIES
Post Office Box 254
Oshkosh, Wisconsin 549002-0254
Telephone: 414-231-6161
Sells coin accessories, and carries one of the largest inventories of "hard to get" and "out of production" coin collecting supplies.

HARRY EDELMAN
111-37 Lefferts Boulevard
Post Office Box 140
South Ozone Park, New York 11420
Telephone: 718-641-2710
Fax: 718-641-0737
Coin holders, books and related supplies.

MOUNT VERNON COIN COMPANY
Post Office Box 672
Annandale, Virginia 22003
Rare Coins and numismatic supplies

DAY MOUNT COMPANY
76 Cummings Circle
West Orange, New Jersey 07052
Telephone: 201-736-7966
Manufactures unique 2x2 flips that do not need to be stapled and are guaranteed to be air tight.

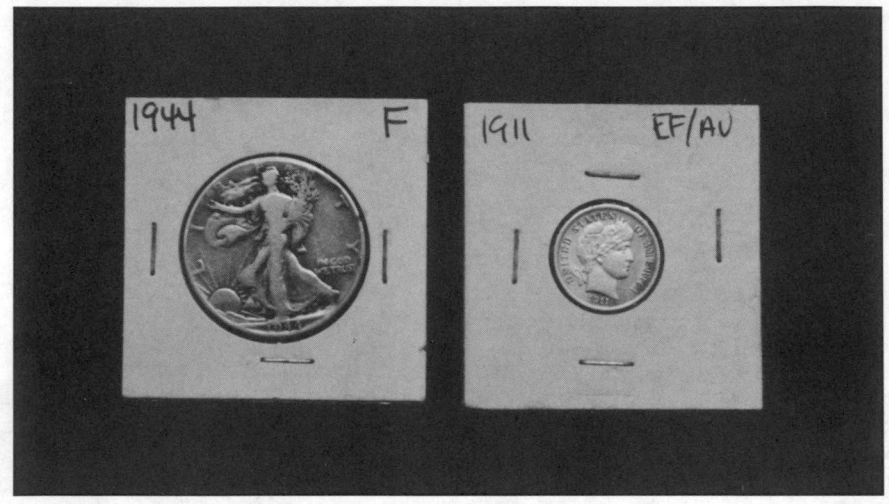

2 x 2's should be used for short term storage only . . . .

COIN PERIODICALS & PUBLICATIONS

COIN WORLD (Newspaper)
Post Office Box 150
Sidney, Ohio 45365
Phone: 800-253-0812
Fax: 513-498-0812
PUBLISHED: Weekly
SINGLE COPY PRICE: $1.95
SUBSCRIPTION: $28 Year

NUMISMATIC NEWS (Newspaper)
700 East State Street
Iola, Wisconsin 54990
Phone: 715-445-2214
PUBLISHED: Weekly
SINGLE COPY PRICE: $1.75
SUBSCRIPTION: $27.95 Year

THE NUMISMATIST (Magazine)
818 North Cascade Avenue
Colorado Springs, Colorado 80903

COINS (Magazine)
700 East State Street
Iola, Wisconsin 54990
Phone: 715-445-2214
PUBLISHED: Monthly
SINGLE COPY PRICE: $2.95
SUBSCRIPTION: $21.95 Year

COIN PRICES
700 East State Street
Iola, Wisconsin 54990
Phone: 715-445-2214
PUBLISHED: Bi-Monthly
SINGLE COPY PRICE: $3.25
SUBSCRIPTION: $16.95 Year

INTANGIBLES

POSITIVE THINKING

If you are to be a successful coinshooter you must also be an optimistic individual. The power of positive thinking is more than just a theory....it actually works! See yourself returning home with valuable, old coins, and you more than likely will. Venture out troubled or despondent and you will surely come home empty handed.

Take care of any pressing business, family obligations or important tasks before going out in the field with your detector. Know that when you hear that threshold hum in your headphones you are in good stead with the

> *"Know that when you hear that ole threshold hum in your headphones, you are in good stead with the world."*

world, free of nagging or demanding obligations. In the process you will feel good about your day, and most of all about your chances of success. A good frame of mind is important to a successful day in the field.

"WE ALL HOPE FOR THE BEST
BUT AN OPTIMIST ACTUALLY EXPECTS TO GET IT!"

DEFINE YOUR GOALS

Whether a seasoned treasure hunter or not, if you want to find older, more valuable coins you must set goals for yourself, and do all you can to meet them. Know precisely what you are after, go for it, and develop a mindset that anything less is failure. Newer clad coins are everywhere, and we know that finding them is easy. If however they are all you seek put this book down and head to the nearest school yard. You will surely come home happy and with a pocket full .... very spendable but not very collectable!

Always set goals for each outing! Putting such demands on yourself results in that extra effort, and ultimately greater satisfaction. Anything worthwhile in life takes extra effort! I try and achieve something, no matter how small or seemingly insignificant every day of my life. Enjoyment for me is thinking about tomorrow, looking ahead and planning my next outing with my detector.......selecting my site and deciding just what I might need to do to find the treasures I seek...... never wondering IF I will be successful, but HOW successful I will be!

If you are serious about coin hunting you know the types of coins you want to find. You also have a pretty good idea of what your town or locale can offer. Put these known factors together, develop a plan and get down to business! When I lived on the east coast one of my goals was to find the 1877 Indian Cent, a coin I needed to complete my collection of that variety. Though I searched many sites that could have given up this key coin I never found it. Now that I live in Texas my goals have changed. I have had to adjust them somewhat backward because Texas does not date back as far as New Jersey does, and because I now deal with the "black gumbo" soil of Dallas......a clay that becomes "muck" in the spring and like "rock" in the dry months of summer. As a result the types of coins I seek are newer, but my goals are still lofty......a 1914D Lincoln or the ever elusive 1916D Mercury dime. I feel certain I will succeed.

As far as I am concerned there are three important prerequisites to being a successful coinshooter.....

1. Have the best equipment available and know how to use it
2. Have a positive outlook, be alert and aware when searching.
3. Research every site adequately....if not it won't matter if you are honoring the first two prerequisites....you won't find coins where they don't exist!.

MAKING THE MOST OF YOUR TIME

One intangible, and yet very important aspect of your coin hunting is knowing that you've given every outing your best effort. Give 120%, and if you come home empty handed you will at least know you probably erred in your research (not in your search). Not giving an outing your very best effort will result in nagging doubts, hindsight, and in most instances a return search of the site. While this may not seem too unreasonable to you it's indicative that you didn't review your options and utilize all of your weapons the first time around.....time is precious, especially when coinhunting is a sideline and/or hobby. Make the best use of your time in the field, and give every outing your undivided attention....it <u>will</u> pay off down the road.

*"A PESSIMIST HAS NO MOTOR;
AN OPTIMIST HAS NO BRAKES!"*

MOTHER NATURE

Mother nature will also play a big part in your success as a coinshooter, and knowing how will make a big difference in your finds. We all know dry, clay like soil, or severe drought conditions make detecting deep targets extremely difficult. Likewise excessive wetness and/or muddy conditions make recovery messy and problematic. The middle ground of course is preferable, but not very predictable or consistently realistic. Dealing with wet, dry, hard, soft, hot and cold is life, and what we must contend with. How to handle each of these scenarios is what we must understand and go with.

Damp or wet ground will always increases a detector's depth capabilities. Knowing this, knowing our past success at a given site, and knowing what techniques we employed at that site can make a world of difference in what we come home with in the future. Let me explain.....

I once hunted an old one room school site back in New Jersey, and had moderate success. I recovered a few old coins,....Indian Head cents, a liberty nickel or two and three Barber dimes. Nothing great, but decent finds nonetheless. I tried using my ten inch coil to gain an inch or two, and also tried my sniper coil to get into the nooks and crannies, but finally assumed that I had found all there was to be found.

Later that summer I went back to the site after two days of heavy rain, and it seemed as though I was hunting the site for the first time. I began finding not only Barber, but Liberty Seated coins and Shield Nickels like they were going out of style. Where had I gone wrong before? The answer of course was the added dampness or moisture in the soil, not any oversight. Likewise I continued to find good coins at this site, but <u>only</u> when the conditions were good, or when Mother Nature said go do your thing! I don't try to explain or understand why wet soil improves my odds.....I just know it does and timing can be all important to your results as well!

"THOSE THAT WAIT FOR OPPORTUNITIES TO TURN UP USUALLY FIND THEMSELVES TURNED DOWN!"

SUDDEN CHANGE

What is sudden change? Sudden change is something that happens without warning, offering only a quick opportunity to detect and find coins. It might be construction work that eliminated sidewalks in an older section of town, or it might be that heavy rain or downpour that ended the drought. It might be the hurricane that took away two feet of sand at the beach, or a flood that carried with it many inches of topsoil. Whatever the sudden change, you the coinshooter, must be alert and be ready to act.

> *"Keep your batteries fresh, your detector ready, and look for sudden change . . . it's around you almost everyday, but it's up to you to notice it and to act."*

While living in New Jersey I actually looked forward to storms that came up the east coast. "Northeasters" were usually damaging storms. Abusive, dramatic and almost always destructive, BUT they almost always generated great detecting. It was not uncommon to meet all your metal detecting friends at the beach either during a hurricane or immediately after. There was even a network of sorts that put the word out about the potential for beach erosion and heavy tides. I was notified by friends on the coast, and I in turn started calling others in my area to get ready for a drive to the shore. Sound crazy? Not if you lived near the ocean, and owned a metal detector. Coastal storms brought in coins and valuables that were previously out of reach, and in turn took sand off the beach, exposing what had before been too deep to detect! The best of both worlds for the treasure hunter......

Sudden change could also be the bulldozing of that old house down the street, the surface grading being done to the old ball field, or the draining of the local lake. It almost always means being ready on a moment's notice to detect an area that may only be available for a few hours.

No matter what the situation, be ready to act on any sudden or unexpected event. Keep your batteries fresh, your detector ready, and be prepared to reap the rewards. These changes occur almost every day, but it's up to you to notice them and to act!

"LUCK IS WHAT HAPPENS WHEN PREPARATION MEETS OPPORTUNITY!"

THE LEAST OBVIOUS

If you approach a particular site that has been hunted heavily in the past, work the <u>least obvious areas</u>; those spots that others would have overlooked, ignored or deemed unworthy. Areas like the most direct path from a vehicle to the center of attraction. . . under bushes or heavy vegetation. . . around the roots and base of a tree. . . the outer, overgrown perimeter of the site, . . . the answer is obvious! Because those before did not.

RESEARCH . . . . THE KEY TO YOUR SUCCESS

Research is without a doubt the single, most important aspect of your success as a coinshooter and treasure hunter. Without accurate information, and detailed preparation you will be wasting your time. Yes I know you have a metal detector, and that you are able to find coins, but if you are not searching in the right places you will not find "those coins" that offer the greatest return on your time. Finding these old and prime sites before the competition is the key!

Research is obtaining information, and information is a universal need. Knowing where to look for it, and how to interpret it is your goal. Information comes from not only books and magazines, but from reading letters or newspaper articles; talking to people and senior citizens of your community, or overhearing a conversation. You'll find useful information in libraries, record

> *"Research is really obtaining information, and information is a universal need. Knowing where to look for it, and how to interpret it is your goal."*

centers, city, county and state offices, museums, public corporations, private organizations and personal files.

I'm not sure why, but the word *research* has a connotation that's misleading. It somehow implies "boring" when in fact it's exciting, and quite often more so than the actual hunt itself. Searching for information is sometimes one surprise after another, with leads and clues turning up to spur you on to the next level. Yes it can be slow and tedious at times, but understanding the overall process can make it a lot easier. You must constantly be thinking "what information might turn up today that will provide me with old coins tomorrow?" Reading, analyzing and putting the pieces of the puzzle together is a lot of fun, especially when you hit paydirt!

This old schoolhouse in rural East Texas was found by reading a local newspaper from 1935, and from talking to the older residents living in the area . . . .

Research itself should be an adjunct of your coinshooting efforts, and a pleasant one...... something to look forward to on a rainy day. Something to work hard on during the winter months (if you live in areas where seasonal weather conditions interfere with your outdoor activities). It keeps the juices going, especially when you come across useful information, compile it and make plans. Winter is ideal for driving the highways and backroads, looking for potential sites, or merely confirmation of your hunches. It's also a great time of the year to seek out landowners, and request permission to hunt their area at a later time.

Last but not least let's not make this subject something monumental. Research to the coinhunter is not like doing a thesis. It's simply finding those places where people congregated, and where, hopefully, they also lost money. You do not have to have a doctorate to accomplish this....merely a little common sense, and a whole lot of perserverance.

"IT'S WHAT WE LEARN AFTER WE KNOW IT ALL THAT REALLY COUNTS"

REVIEW & REAFFIRMATION

When you decided to purchase a metal detector you surely had places in mind to search. You kept thinking of that vacant lot across town where you played ball as a kid. You thought about the house and homesite where you grew up that is now nothing more than a field, and you had visions of riches when you thought you were the only one to remember the old carnival area just outside town. All good and very noble reasons to buy a metal detector, but chances are few of these sites proved productive. You learned that the areas in question did not really hold as many coins as you thought.

These assumptions and/or dreams of wealth achieved a purpose. They got you involved in a pastime that was fun, and that made you learn how to use a metal detector. They taught you that old coins are only there for the taking if you do your home-work, and they taught you that you must find newer and more productive areas to detect. Most important they taught you never to assume you were the only one privy to a given area or site. You were not the only one with a metal detector and dreams of riches!!

The question now is what are you going to do to correct this situation? You can continue to hunt the school yard or the corner lot, but don't you long for those very old and often valuable coins? Of course you do! So what's stopping you? The answer of course is you are reluctant to put forth the effort to find them.

We're all creatures of habit, and one of our most popular habits is opting for the path of least resistance, the most obvious....... the most accessible! If it's simple and easy we do it. If it involves effort we put it off. Well my friends, that doesn't work when it comes to coin hunting. Every time you put off doing your homework you lose another site to the detectorist who has done his! Continue this pattern and you will surely be left in the dust!

> "Everytime you put off doing your homework you lose another site to the detectorist who is doing his! Continue this practice and you will surely be left in the dust."

If you think that by reading this book you will discover some overlooked, obscure, long secreted, metal detector setting or technique that will let you find those deeper coins, forget it!! Such information is not within these pages, or for that matter in any other metal detecting book I've read over the past twenty years. Metal detecting....coin hunting is hard work! What makes it palatable is that it's fun, and if you want to work a little and have fun at the same time....read on.

Forget about your first forays in the field.....they are history. Accept the fact that you must find new areas to detect. Also accept the fact that you need to know more about your town, your county and your state, and that you must get more from your equipment. You remembered the early sites, you took what they had to offer, but now you must move on. It's time for greener pastures!

A productive coin site is not that difficult to define. It's an area that was used by hundreds or maybe even thousands of people for a long period of time, and has never been searched with a metal detector. A fantastic scenario right? Maybe, but such sites <u>do exist</u>, and they are your goal! Are there many like this out there? Absolutely! Finding them however is up to you. The process is not easy, but with a little fortitude, dedication, good research and hard work you will be successful!

"GOOD LUCK IS A LAZY MAN'S ESTIMATE OF A WORKERS SUCCESS"

THE ELECTRONIC REVOLUTION

As of this writing computers, and in particular computer networks, are becoming the buzz word in Americana. Netware, Internet, the Information Highway are the "in words", and as we continue this techno-trend, the future of research, and the availability of materials to you, the coinhunter, will surely increase ten fold Electronic know-how, and the computer in partcicular, have made the 90's the era of easily accessible materials and information. We are in an era that will surely be remembered in time as one of the most progressive and one of the most important in technological history. As a result you should be the beneficiary!

No longer do we need to leave our homes, drive long distances to obtain the information we need. We only have to have an up-to-date computer, a modem and related programs to access the many contacts that are important to our search. While somewhat new to us now, I suspect that in five years this technology will be second nature to us....only time will tell.

THE LIBRARY

To begin your research work visit your library. <u>Books provide information....libraries provide books.</u> Libraries are not what they used to be...they're constantly changing and for the better, especially since the early 1970's. More books, pamphlets and newspapers are being copied onto microfilm, computer disks and these formats allow libraries and other similiar organizations to buy more information and store it in less space. Instead of traveling hundreds of miles to use certain materials the same information is as close as your local library.

Larger libraries do not simply have more of the same things that smaller libraries have, and libraries, contrary to popular belief, do not have <u>every</u> book published, nor do they all buy the same titles. Whether it's a public library, an academic library, a community college library, a public library or a museum library......each offers different titles to help you in your search for older coins.

THE PUBLIC LIBRARY

Public libraries come in all sizes and offer varied services to the coinhunter. Most neighborhood branches of a large library system maintain small, but often useful collections of reference books. They are also more flexible than the main library and will frequently lend magazines and other periodicals since they only hold on to them for a couple of years. The <u>branch</u> library can also serve as a bridge or an intermediary in dealing with other libraries. You

> *"Larger libraries do not simply have more of the same things that smaller libraries have, and libraries, contrary to popular belief, do not buy every book published, nor do they all buy the same titles."*

can reserve and receive materials from other, sometimes, better stocked libraries. Most all libraries today are connected by computer and it is not difficult for one library to access the other's database, saving a lot of time and wasted gas.

Many of the smaller libraries also have regional files, covering events, history and services unique to their area. They might consist of postcards, pictures, centennial publications, maps, old phone books, old newspapers, posters, and private diaries and letters from citizens of the community. These "homegrown" files are unique and extremely valuable to you as a coin hunter. Study them closely, and record the data you find.

STATE LIBRARIES

State libraries are found in all fifty states, and while they are set up to serve state government, they also share materials with public libraries. They often have special research collections available to the public. If you live closeby one of these libraries be sure to find out what they have to offer. When I lived in New Jersey I frequently visited the state library in Trenton, and profited greatly from information I found there...

ACADEMIC LIBRARIES

The very thought of visiting a college or university library probably scares you. It shouldn't! Don't let the formal setting and large volumes of material intimidate you. Many academic libraries offer <u>unrestricted</u> use of their services, and a few offer fee cards which allow you to check out books (Prices can range from $10 to $100 per year). Call those in your area to find out their policies, and remember interlibrary loan is one way to <u>avoid paying a fee</u>.

Unlike public libraries that buy new books to serve the general public, academic libraries usually cater to researchers, buying those books that are out of print, and that cover every topic imaginable. They also have a much larger and more complete collection of history books than does the public library. It is advisable to check the major courses of study offered at the local colleges in your area to determine their subject strengths.

A good rule of thumb is to use the largest library you can find for your research. More often than not it will be an academic library...not the local public branch. Another advantage is that academic libraries are usually open on weekends and late at night....<u>perfect</u> if you work during the day.

THE LIBRARY OF CONGRESS

As the name implies this library serves the members of Congress. It is however the national library of the United States, and as such is available to you. The library of Congress is the largest library in the world with over 100 million items (20 million of them books)! The LC, if you did not know, has a copy of every book ever printed here in the United States. This is part of the copyright process. The difficulty with this institution is that their materials are non-circulating.

One of the LC's contributions to the many smaller libraries however is the cataloging it provides for materials. It also distributes them electronically, so be sure you inquire about this potential aid at your local library. You can also write: LIBRARY OF CONGRESS, 10 First Street SE, Washington, D.C. 20540.

LIBRARIES OF THE FUTURE

One can only imagine what the libraries in 2001 will be like. With computer technology advancing at unbelievable increments it's certainly possible there will not be any physical libraries per se.

Computer networks, databases and information sharing makes what was once fairly complicated now rather simple. I suspect you will be able to obtain all the information you need without ever leaving the confines of your home.

KNOW WHEN & HOW
TO ASK FOR HELP

Never be afraid to ask for assistance when you are researching. Find the research librarian, and explain what you are after. State your goal, your current problem (if any), and exactly what information you currently have, no matter how insignificant it may seem to you at the time. Remember.....not telling the whole story or giving incomplete information will result in an incomplete or wrong answer.

Understand also that the research librarian is a busy person, and do all you can to cultivate his or her friendship. Over time they might develop an interest in your hobby, and in helping you find those older coin sites that exist in the area. Let me also state however that when possible DO YOUR OWN RESEARCH! Finding the clues yourself is more rewarding and adds to the overall enjoyment of your pastime. You also become more aware of your goals, and will usually take more notice of things that the uninitiated would ignore or gloss over.

"IT IS A GOOD BOOK
WHEN IT IS OPENED WITH EXPECTATIONS
AND CLOSED WITH DELIGHT & PROFIT"

HISTORICAL SOCIETY LIBRARIES

Historical societies are located in most every community in the United States. They vary in organization and size from being a loose knit group of historically minded citizens with little research experience, but lots of time to man the library, to well funded groups with skilled historians, and possibly even a full time librarian. Whatever their makeup these groups focus on the history of the area, and this is precisely the information you are after. Area historical societies have documents and original materials found nowhere else.....diaries kept by community residents, company account books, ledgers, photos, newspaper clippings, family histories, artifacts and much, much more. Old records and documents are often donated to area historical societies when individuals die, companies go out of business or when schools close or move.

Remember however that historical societies usually keep somewhat erratic hours so be sure to call ahead if you intend to make use of their materials. Also if it appears that a historical society has a great deal to offer you may want to consider membership. Annual fees are usually reasonable, and many such groups offer members free library privileges and other benefits, such as lectures, workshops and trips.

ORGANIZATION IS A MUST

All of the above suggestions, ideas or theories will certainly save you time and effort in your research, but the most important aspect of this information gathering is organization! Notes are useless if they cannot be deciphered or understood! When you are recording information be accurate and write clearly. Be sure you spell words correctly, especially the names of individuals and locales (streets, roads, etc.). Use only one side of a page, and always record the source from which you got that information. Include the page number, the author, title and the library from which you borrowed the book. Copy anything and everything that will help you locate the information again if you need it.

Not only be careful with names and addresses, but be careful with initials. You will frequently find many of the same family inhabit a community or county, and often first names will be the same. Middle initials or nicknames might be the only way to locate the exact one you are looking for! Finally keep a record of the sources you've tried, even if you've found nothing. This will save you from repeating the same effort later on, and should you seek help or turn the research over to someone else they'll want to know what you've already read and researched.

INTERLIBRARY LOAN

If a particular title or book is not available from your local library ask about whether or not they are able to obtain it from another one. Interlibrary loan (ILL) is fairly common today, and ideal for the researcher. Most libraries participate in this program, but keep in mind there might be a fee for the service. Ask first.

Most interlibrary requests are sent by computer from the main branch library. The librarian types the author and title of the book you've requested, and seconds later a full bibliographic description of the book appears, followed by a list of libraries nationwide that own copies of the book! Almost 6,000 US libraries participate in this computerized system called OCLC (On-Line Computer Library Center, Inc.). The database is enormous and quite useful to all of the members.

REFERENCE BOOKS

A great deal of your coinhunting research will be reading reference books (almanacs, directories, old maps, documents and diaries and rare area history books). Most of these items cannot be checked out, and must be read "at" the library, but never assume that this is always the case. It never hurts to ask for something if you need it. Sometimes a reference librarian will make an exception and loan a book overnight, with the understanding that it is to be returned first thing in the morning.

NEWSPAPERS

Newspapers, especially very old ones are extremely useful to your coinhunting efforts. These publications, once thought of as disposable, are now an important part of historical America, offering the only day-to-day accounting of our existence.

Local, county and statewide newspapers are now preserved on microfilm or floppy disk, and can provide details of what happened years ago in your area. Inquire at your local and county newspaper offices about making use of their archives.

While perusing these old newspapers be on the lookout for social teas, sporting events, and church programs. Years ago these happenings were advertised, promoted and preserved in the local tabloid. They are all of value to the coinhunter and should be pursued. Because they attracted people, they should be considered as "potential" sites.

Since old newspapers are not indexed, finding the useful information will often be hit and miss. Do however seek out issues that were published just after major holidays such as Memorial Day, July 4th and Labor Day. They will often detail how people celebrated and most important, where. Needless to say photos are a real plus!

Reading obituaries in old newspapers can also be interesting. The information given differs from what is printed today. It's personal, and will surprise you by it's thoroughness. I have found more than a few mentions of how wealthy residents died, leaving spouses and heirs penniless. The implication is almost always that the individuals savings were buried or hidden somewhere.

Old newspapers are not only available at the newspapers office, but often at the local library. Ask your reference librarian about this service, and be sure to make use of it. It is one of the most useful, and one of the most overlooked tools of the coinhunter

"A SMALL TOWN NEWSPAPER IN TEXAS ADVERTISED,"READ YOUR BIBLE TO KNOW WHAT PEOPLE OUGHT TO DO. READ THIS PAPER TO KNOW WHAT THEY ACTUALLY DO"

WHAT TO LOOK FOR

Learning how to effectively research may take some time, but once you understand how to do it you will find it a very easy process. Random, unorganized efforts result in hit or miss answers and finds, and a lot of wasted time! They're also extremely frustrating!

No matter what the task facing us, we usually learn by doing, and researching good coin sites is no different. Define and know your goal, do your homework, and you will reap the rewards. Once you have a plan of action, the information you seek will come.   When others ask me about how to start their researching I always suggest they begin by reading books that are fun, easy to read, and that will often offer a few quick leads. What types of books am I talking about? Centennial and Sesqui-Centennial Celebration booklets quickly come to mind, as do old school yearbooks. They're filled with old photos, and usually provide immediate returns to an attentive reader......just what you need to get your effort into overdrive! Community celebration booklets document the many events that took place over the years, and in many instances do it chronologically, allowing you to go back to those years or periods when certain key or semi-key coins may have been lost with more frequency.

Some celebrations or events may have attracted hundreds, possibly thousands, while others only a few. Some were enjoyed each year over a long period, while others occurred only once or twice. While all hold some potential put those that attracted the largest number of people on top of your list. An event, held only once, attracting five thousand people, will offer as much a return on your time as one that was held each year for ten years, but only attracted a hundred or so each time.

As you continue to read, try to determine when and where the first schools were built; the first factories, the first businesses and the first taverns. Did a railroad pass through your community?

If so where was the local passenger station? Was there a black-smith shop, a market, or a farmers co-op?

Read and read some more and find out what sort of recreation was popular in your region early on, and where it took place? Did your community sponsor a baseball team? A football team? If so, where did they play their games? Where were the weekend resorts and campgrounds in your county? Where did the traveling circus set up it's tents, and where was the carnival held each year? Was there a local amusement park that attracted people? The bottom line.....what exactly did people do to enjoy themselves? What activities did they participate in that might have caused them to lose money (coins of course)? Did they drive to the coast and to the beach in the summer? Did they frequent the picnic groves in the area....did they spend their Sundays listening to the band concerts in the park? The questions you must ask are endless, and the answers are your beginning to great coinhunting.

What steep hill did the kids at the turn of the century take their sleds to? Where are the ole swimming holes that offered relief during the long hot summers? Was there a vacant lot somewhere in town that sufficed for the neighborhood baseball or football game, and was there a favorite fishing spot along the river or creek? Assuming there were boy scouts in your town years ago......where did they spend summer camp?

Read to find out where the oldest parts of the community are. Seek out those senior citizens living today who can provide you with in-person assistance. Read to better appreciate and to under-stand what folks a hundred years ago gathered together to do. Understand and always remember that things were very different back then. What we take for granted today was in all likelihood far fetched 100 years ago. You must begin to think old to find the old. And lastly...to spur you on a little more....imagine, if you will, that "key" coin you seek was simply pocket change back then!

There will be many rewarding sites that will take time to

locate, and these will almost always outproduce those that were obvious. Why? Very simply if the area was obvious to you it was obvious to other detectorists. This is not to imply however that you should not detect it. Go for it, and never assume anything! The hard to define or hard to find site however will almost always produce in unimaginable ways.....the extra effort is definitely worth it!

REFERENCE BOOKS TO ASSIST YOU

Now that you know about the various libraries that might be of help in your research, how do you find out what's around you, and which might be the best for your efforts. The following publications can help:

1. *THE AMERICAN LIBRARY DIRECTORY*, published by R.R. Bowker and Company (Annual)
This is an alphabetical by state list of approximately 30,000 U.S. and Canadian libraries: public, academic, company, museum, newspaper, special subject, private, historical society, church, bank, military, government, law, association and much more.

   This publication will also indicate budget size, and subject strengths for each of the above.

2. *DIRECTORY OF HISTORICAL SOCIETIES AND AGENCIES IN THE UNITED STATES & CANADA.* Published every three years by The American Association for State and Local History.

   A geographical list of historical and genealogical societies with addresses.

3. *SUBJECT COLLECTIONS*, Published by R.R. Bowker and Company (published approximately every five to seven years).
   This directory is arranged by subject only. It identifies the subject collections in 7,000 academic public, museum and historical society libraries nationwide.

4. *TREASURES OF THE LIBRARY OF CONGRESS*, by Charles A. Goodrum.
   Published in 1991 this book has a lot of illustrations, and lists the LC's rare collections...books, photographs, prints, maps and manuscripts....

5. *THE WHOLE LIBRARY CATALOG HANDBOOK, BY* George M. Eberhart.
   Also published in 1991 you'll find current data, professional advice and curiosa about libraries and libary services.

GOVERNMENT PRINTING OFFICE

The United States Government is actually the world's largest publisher, based on the sheer number of documents it prints. Many of these government publications are offered to the public directly or through libraries, and most are free or available at very reasonable fees. What types of information might this agency provide you in your efforts....? How about reports on schools, colleges, universities, old forts, military bases, battlesites, recreational areas and early railroads?

The best place to start searching for government publications is your local library. Libraries often carry large numbers of government documents, either because a diligent librarian has collected them, or because the library itself has been designated as a depository through the Federal Depository Library program. This program was established by Congress to provide free access to government publications. As a result 1400 libraries maintain large collections of government publications, 53 of which are regional depository libraries (carrying complete collections).

For a listing of these regional libraries write: Federal Depository Library Program, U.S. GOVERNMENT PRINTING OFFICE, Superintendent of Documents, Washington, D.C. 20402. When writing also request a Subject Bibiograpby Index....it is free and will detail all of the specific subject bibilographies that are available.

MAPS

If you are to be a successful coinhunter begin collecting maps of your community, your county, your area and your state, that will enhance your chances of finding old coins. Most any map or platte will be useful and referenced over and over again. Old or new, detailed or general, maps play a major role in your coinhunting forays. They are documents that detail, and that are usually reliable. As you continue to read and research clues and references to old coinsites will turn up again and again.... your maps will take you to them.

Older maps or plats (as they were called) are even more useful to the coinhunter because they offer a glimpse of the past.....a layout and design of how your community looked years ago. Where the "gathering" places were, where the action was, and more importantly, where you should detect today. These early maps can often be found at your local or county library. You can find them at flea markets, garage sales or auctions. Wherever, and whenever.... look for them....they will pay big dividends down the road.

Maps of any area change over time, sometimes dramatically, and as these changes take place you will become more and more knowledgeable about the area in question. Change is constant, and as coinhunters we must continue to be aware of changes that take place. Paths will become roads, and roads become highways. Villages grow into small towns, communities and sometimes big cities. Seemingly obvious coin sites disappear, and sometimes comparisons of old and new will often bring them back to life.

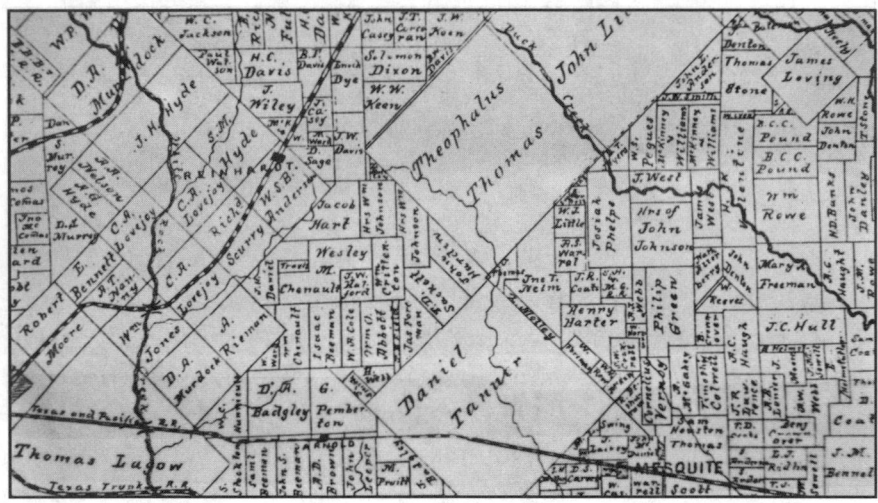

Old maps were drawn up to indicate who owned what, and as such are invaluable when lookng for forgotten sites like Johnson's Grove, Tanner's Distillery, Ludlow's Blacksmith Shop or Levi's Tavern.

Maps are outlines....descriptions if you will, of geographical locations....drawn and designed to help people travel to destinations unknown. Treasure sites? Possibly! They indicate the quickest routes, the most direct and frequently offer additional clues if you know where you are heading. If you have a plan, a purpose and a general direction, a map can and will often make the difference, taking you there instantly. Know where you are going, what you are after, and things will fall into place.

TOPOGRAPHICAL MAPS

Without a doubt the most important map in your arsenal will be the <u>TOPOGRAPHICAL MAP.</u> Topographical maps are available from the United States Department of the Interior, and are often instant sources for finding old, valuable coins. "Topo" maps (as they are called) are precise, detailed and a must if you are to be a productive coinhunter.

Topo maps are available in various scales and sizes, but the *7.5 minute series is best.* The scale is one inch to 2000 feet, and the area that is covered is from 49 to 71 square miles. It offers good detail and a real feel for the physical locale. These maps are in color with landmark indications and symbols for schools, churches, campgrounds, racetracks, railroads, mines, rivers, creeks, and much, much more. You will find yourself referring to these detailed maps over and over again as you continue your coinhunting efforts.

Topography is defined as "the science of representing the surface features of a region on maps and charts", and while your sought after treasures lie beneath the surface remember it's what's on top that will always lead you to it. Topo maps may be purchased from map dealers in your area, but if not write to the following government agencies:

IF YOU LIVE EAST OF THE MISSISSIPPI

U.S. Department of the Interior
U.S. Geological Survey
907 National Center
Reston, Virgina 22092

IF YOU LIVE WEST OF THE MISSISSIPPI

U.S. Department of the Interior
U.S. Geological Survey
Box 25286/Federal Center
Denver, Colorado 80115

Topographical maps are probably your best resource for finding old coins . . . . Find them, study them, and let them lead you to where they are!

When you write to these agencies indicate the state and county maps needed, and request all materials that relate to them. After you have topo maps of your areas try and find those that came before. Older ones are around. Many are available from map dealers, and reasonable in price. They could be photocopies, and in fact probably will be, but this is not a problem. Major roads, streams and landmarks will help you match the old with the new, and allow for fairly easy cross reference.

By comparing the old with the new you will instantly find productive coin sites. You will notice landmarks on the earlier map that are not on the more recent one, indicating perhaps a homesite that has disappeared, an old one room school that was torn down, or maybe a pond area that has been filled in. You might also notice that the one room school house has now become a private residence, or that the old scout camp is now apparently just a field or pasture. Map study and comparison is fun, and something that can be accomplished on a rainy day, in the evening or during the winter. Look slowly and look carefully....you'll be surprised at the clues that are present!

MAP INFORMATION & ASSISTANCE

MAP LINK
25 East Mason
Santa Barbara, California 93101
Phone: 805-965-4402
Fax: 805-962-0884
(Map Wholesaler and Retailer with over 85,000 titles in stock. Good source for "hard to find items").

NORTHERN MAP COMPANY
103 Cherokee Circle
Dunnellen, Florida 32630
Phone: 904-489-3967
(Old State, Railroad, County and Civil War Maps).

GEORGRAPHY & MAP DIVISION
Library of Congress
Washington, D. C. 20402
(You name it....they have it.
Request listing of those available for duplication and mail
ing).

OKLAHOMA TREASURE TRADERS
5378 27TH Place
Tulsa, Oklahoma 74114
(Handles older topographical maps)

K.B. SLOCUM BOOKS/MAPS
Post Office Box 620
Austin, Texas 78766
Phone: 512-258-7442
(Large selection of treasure hunting books and maps).

ACCESS MAPS & GEAR
321 S. Guadalupe
Santa Fe, New Mexico 87501
Phone: 505-982-3330
(Interesting selection of maps and and accessories).

UNITED STATES GOVERNMENT PRINTING OFFICE
Superintendent of Documents
Washington, D.C. 20402
(Maps & Atlases)

ARMY CORPS OF ENGINEERS
Public Affairs
Army Corps of Engineers
Dept. of Defense
20 Massachusetts Ave. NW
Room 1101
Washington, D.C. 20314
Phone: 202-272-0011
(Inland waterway charts and maps of federal recreation lands.
This office will send listing of local offices that can assist you
in your area).

BUREAU OF LAND MANAGEMENT
Eastern States Office
350 South Pickett Street
Alexandria, Virginia 22304
(Plats of townships and mineral surveys. NOTE...If you
happen to live in Illinois, Indiana, Iowa, Kansas, Missour or
Ohio you must write to:
National Archives & Record Administration, Cartographic
Archives Division, Pennsylvania Avenue at 8th Street NW.,
Washington, D.C. 20408)

INTERNATIONAL MAP DEALERS ASSOCIATION
Post Office Box 1789
Kankakee, Illinois 60901
Phone: 815-939-4627
(Can provide names and addresses of map dealers in your
area).

YOUR EQUIPMENT

USING YOUR DETECTOR TO THE MAX

Most of us think we know our metal detector inside out; after all we've used it for many years haven't we...? While that may certainly be true, in the course of pursuing our treasures we usually overlook the obvious, opting for the easiest and most convenient methods of operation, rationalizing any unsuccessful outing by saying the site was cleaned out! After all we spent four or five hours hunting; if old coins were there we would have found them right? <u>WRONG!</u>

A metal detector is an electronic instrument manufactured to detect the presence of metal, but like any other electronic piece of equipment it has certain capabilities and limita-

> *"We usually overlook the obvious, opting for the easiest and most convenient, rationalizing any successful outing by saying the site was cleaned out!"*

tions, and a good understanding of what they are is important. For example....do you set each and every control on your detector to maximize it's overall effectiveness and efficiency in every given situation or do you opt for a preset program? Do you assume erratic signals and chatter are indicative of a worthless item? Do you know whether or not the ground in the area you are hunting is positive or negative? I think we both know the answers to these questions. The point I'm trying to make....as no two faces are alike, no two sites are alike, each one demanding a well thought out approach, plan of action and an individualized metal detector setting.

WHY DETECTOR SETTINGS ARE IMPORTANT

Your metal detector, no matter the make or model, is a transmitter and receiver. It sends out eddy currents into the soil, and when these currents are interrupted by metal a return signal is sent back to the receiver, causing an audio response that we, as users, must analyze and react to in some way. Simple enough? Not really! What you must remember is that these currents react most noticeably to <u>surface area</u>, not mass.

To better understand this take a quarter... move it back and forth under your detector's searchcoil with the face (flat surface) of the coin parallel to the coil. Note the strong signal it produces, even at a distance of eight to ten inches. Now take the quarter, with the "edge" of the coin facing the bottom of the coil and do the same thing. How strong is the audio response now? Begin to move it away from the coil...does the signal become even more difficult to hear? Well if you were to take 8 quarters, hold them together, and perform the same test you would not gain any depth when they were held parallel (face up) to the coil, but you would gain depth when held on <u>edge</u> because the <u>surface area</u> would be greater.

Thus if everything were ideal every coin ever lost would be lying flat in the ground, allowing for easy recovery, but of course this is not the case. Add the problem of fringe area targets, (those just barely outside your scan area), outside interference, weather conditions, soil composition, and you begin to understand the complexity of (1) finding coins below six inches, and (2) cleaning out any site.

How then do you set the controls on your detector when you are after the deep and very old? Do you simply turn it on and set them at the preset marks, assuming that these are the best settings? If so you are wrong! Presets are put on metal detectors so that the beginner or novice can set the controls quickly, and begin using it under "average conditions". They are average settings, and while they're not all that bad they will not give you any edge over the competition (who is probably doing the same thing).

If you happen to own the Eagle Spectrum XLT you are in good stead because this is one metal detector that allows a great deal of fine tuning. It's already extremely deep in it's preset modes, and when you start tweeking the individual functions you are leaps and bounds ahead of the field. The best part of course is that once you find that finely tuned setup you can save it in the user program mode.

I will not spend a great deal of time discussing the Spectrum XLT because all the information you need is in "SPECTRUM ...BETTER DEPTH & PERFORMANCE", written by Darryl Townley, and available at most all Treasure Hunting Stores. Darryl goes into depth about all the many Eagle features, and if you own the XLT you should also own this text.

Now let's consider a few metal detector functions, settings and see how they can affect your efficiency when it comes to finding the deeper coins....

"DON'T FIND FAULT WITH WHAT YOU DON'T UNDERSTAND"

DISCRIMINATION

If you want to find older coins consistently you cannot use high level discrimination...*no if's and's or buts!!* I know you've heard this statement before but it's a fact....overwith and done! To get down to where the better coins are you need every inch of depth possible, and each notch of discrimination used works against you.

You're most likely mumbling "if I reduce my discrimination I'll be digging nothing but trash". Well there's no question you will dig *more* trash, but you will not dig *"only"* trash. In fact the ratio of good to bad will probably surprise you. Remember too that each time you remove a pulltab or two you are opening up another small window, and in the process maybe exposing coins that were masked by the surrounding trash. Is this extra work worth it? You bet! Tedious but productive! My recommendation .....Your discrimination setting should always be a notch below nickel acceptance!

I am quite aware that most nickels found are not worth a great deal because of their metallic makeup and subsequent corrosion. I do however recommend the notch below nickel acceptance because I am not opposed to finding a gold coin, a gold ring or for that matter a nice diamond ring! If you are.....find another pastime! Don't bite off your nose to spite your face! The thoughts of leaving a gold coin in the ground because I was tired really bothers me!

When it comes to the XLT you can obviously reject and accept to your heart's content, however for the most part this is usually not uneccessary. I sometimes make use of the learn reject feature when a particular item of trash is driving me crazy, but by and large I do most of my searching in the coin/jewelry factory program. It's fairly consistant with my "notch below nickel" motto, and it's a program that is not made up of *averages*.....it's one that utilizes engineering know-how, and a lot of in-the field-statistical data. You will dig a little more trash, but you will certainly dig a lot of old coins.

INTUITIVE DISCRIMINATION

Each signal you hear through your headphones needs to be carefully analyzed. Listen not only to the audio response, but note where it reads on your display. Each item will have a characteristic response and readout. Listen, look and make a concerted effort to relate each of them to one another.....it will be time well spent. Do this religiously over a period of time, and you will begin to refine your hearing, and your ability to discern a coin from a pulltab, a dime from a quarter, and a nickel from a penny. No I'm not crazy! Metal detector users who have hunted any length of time will tell you that it's not difficult to develop this skill. You can begin to know trash from treasure.... taking time to analyze before you recover the target is extremely important.....

Let me emphasize again that if you are dead set against digging pulltabs and other similiar trash items, put this book down! You will not find the coins you seek without a little extra effort. Aluminum pulltabs, whether you like it or not, are here to stay, and while they may not be problematic at all sites, they're a nuisance that has to be dealt with. Pull-tabs are lighter, do not sink as quickly as a coin, and as a result will be detected first, causing any coin below it to be ignored. The answer of course is to remove them and allow the better finds to be detected. If the area goes back a few years it

> *"Let me again emphasize that if you are dead set against digging pulltabs and other similar trash items, put this book down!"*

surely holds a few coins you would love to have in your collection. To find them you must be agreeable to working a little harder, even if it means digging more trash! Get the drift?

Searching this old farm site meant constantly fine tuning my detector, but the end result was well worth it!

"DOING NOTHING IS THE MOST TIRESOME JOB IN THE WORLD BECAUSE YOU CAN'T STOP & REST"

SENSITIVITY

Any increase at all in the sensitivity or depth control on your detector will increase your chances of finding better coins, but understand that as you increase it you also increase your detector's sensitivity to trash. Knowing when and how to adjust this control is important to your success as a coin hunter. Your goal should always be to increase the sensitivity as far as possible without receiving erratic operation. When instability does occur, back off just to where audio threshold stabilizes and then use this setting for searching.

It's important to know as well that stability or smoothness of operation means different things to different people. I know of a few friends of mine who can put up with a whole lot of chatter and still analyze the signal coming through. I frequently found that their settings were too much for my ears, and usually opted for a lesser, more stable operating threshold. What you are comfortable with is for you to decide, and depends upon your needs and tolerance level.

Using optimum (but stable) sensitivity will maximize your efforts and often offer the edge you need to succeed in difficult areas. Determining this precise setting is not all that difficult, and worth the time and effort. Minimum discrimination coupled with maximum sensitivity is a potent weapon, and one which will surely beat the hobbyist using the preset factory settings.

On the XLT set your A.C. and D.C. Sensitivity as high as possible for the conditions facing you. Remember however that stability is also important. Fantastic depth coupled with blips, bops, beeps and boops all over the place won't cut it....find that higher setting that offers good stability, and get down to business.

> "Your goal should always be to increase the sensitivity control as far as possible without receiving erratic operation."

THE ALL METAL MODE

We've now discussed how lowering your discrimination and increasing your sensitivity affects your detector's ability to go deeper, but you still have more in your arsenal....the all metal mode! For some reason most detectorists overlook or ignore this mode of operation, assuming I guess that it's only for the prospector? What makes this even more puzzling is that today we have ID meters to supplement our target analysis.

The all metal mode is the deepest mode on your metal detector. When searching in all metal you hear each and every metallic target in the ground, and you will hear them at much greater depths than you will in the discrimination mode. As a result using all metal in an extremely trashy area will be somewhat annoying, but by scanning slowly, and carefully studying your display readouts you can overcome this problem to a great extent. I also recommend "manually" ground balancing in this mode IF your detector offers this option. White's "AUTOTRAC" is without a doubt the finest and most accurate tracking system in the business today, and should be used for 80% of your coinhunting forays, but if you are in an area that seems to be void of any targets whatsoever, try the manual ground balance feature and go over it again. The XLT offers <u>coarse</u> as well as <u>fine</u> adjustments, and they just might make a world of difference in what you come home with! You would never listen to your stereo without fine tuning it....manual ground balancing fine tunes your detector, and allows you to use it to the max.

> *"For some reason most detectorists ignore this mode of operation, assuming I guess that it's only for the prospector."*

TARGET ID METERS

Target ID meters or displays are here to stay, and they are becoming more accurate and dependable each year. What you must remember however is that they are "probable" target identifiers only. Depending too much on what the display tells you can be disastrous, and I speak from experience. Years ago when target ID displays were first introduced I became addicted, trusting the visual readout, ignoring the audio response, and forgetting about the intuitive, gut feelings that had for so long resulted in a great many old and valuable coins. I was sure this new technology would take care of everything. It would not lie! In fact it lulled me into a false sense of security!

> *"Target ID meter or displays are here to stay, and are becoming more accurate and dependable. What you must remember, however, is that they are still "probable" target identifiers only!"*

I have found the Spectrum XLT display, and the 6000 Di meter (pictured above) to be the most accurate on the market today!

Displays, both LCD and metered, are based on signal strength, and when you consider that the coins you are seeking are often very deep you must ask yourself if the interruption in the eddy currents from your searchcoil is going to be strong enough to "trigger" that needle or LCD readout? The answer of course is that it probably won't!!

Gauge <u>your</u> meter's effectiveness by taking coins of various denominations and passing them underneath your searchcoil, watching the meter's response. Hold them on edge, hold them an inch away, and hold them six inches away, and as you do this note how your meter reacts. At what point does it cease to identify the coin accurately? At what point does it not respond at all? By doing this you will quickly understand why you cannot rely on your ID meter alone for finding the deeper coins.

I do like Target ID displays, and feel certain that eventually they will prove even more predictable and accurate. The Spectrum XLT readout is without question the best on the market today. The target signature it produces is multi-faceted, more detailed than what the competiton offers, and as a result the percentage of trash dug has been reduced almost to nothing! I must however continue to remind myself that the display is <u>still a secondary analysis of the target</u> in the ground. First and foremost I listen to the audio, and base my decision to dig on that and that alone. If my ID display does not agree with the audio indications or my "gut feeling" I dig the target, and let me assure you that more often than not my gut feeling is the right one!

TONAL OR BI-LEVEL AUDIO

A few metal detectors offer bi-level audio responses (or in the case of the XLT...mixed mode audio) that can sometimes assist in defining a target. Typically a lower audio response means trash, and a higher one a coin or some sort of "better" target. This type of audio discrimination is fine when you are searching for shallow coins at a site that has very little trash. You will recover only good targets, but you will surely overlook the deeper coins. Using this feature for an initial search of a site is fine, but sooner or later you will exhaust the area of surface coins, and will need to go deeper. When this happens turn this feature off!! Just as the very deep coin will not trigger a target ID meter, neither will it trigger this audio feature.

The Mixed Mode Audio is, by it's very nature, a noisy mode. A year or two ago it was phased out on earlier Eagle models, and was brought back because relic hunters liked the depth they received from it. Be extra careful however adjusting your AC and DC Sensitivity with this mode...it's typically a little unstable, and increasing its sensitivity will only add to the problem.

THRESHOLD

Utilizing a constant audio threshold is something I will not waver on and for good reason. Over the years I have tried a few models of metal detectors offering "silent" operation.

This Barber Half Dollar was found at a depth of about 12 inches and produced only a very minute inflection in my audio threshold!

While these detectors were sometimes very good I was not able to find the deeper coins with them (compared to those offering minimal audio threshold), and the reason, I believe, is easy to understand.

As deep coins do not give off strong enough signals to trigger target IDs, or audio identifiers, neither will they give sufficient signal strength to "break" through the silent mode of operation.

Often however, these "same" targets will cause fluctuation in your threshold sound. This fluctuation will often be slight, but obvious if you are listening! You will have to be very attentive, but that's something you should be doing anyway. Any miniscule increase or variance in your threshold almost always indicates a very deep target, and it matters not what it is, if you are after the better coins you must recover it.

Setting my threshold to where it's just barely audible is routine, and when I'm faced with a lot of outside noise (traffic, people, wind, etc.) I will even turn it up a notch or two. No, I don't particularly like the constant hum, but I do like knowing I will hear any inflection or increase that takes place when I walk over that old seated dime at eight to ten inches. Most all old coin signals will be weak, and only an acutely trained ear will hear them. <u>I cannot emphasize enough the need to listen, rather that watch!!</u>

S.A.T. SPEED

If you own a White's model metal detector you more than likely have the ability to control your "Self Adjusting Threshold" speed. What does this feature do? Well it controls how fast your detector resets it's threshold after rejecting a target. This procedure may take a second or two, and if you happen to be searching an extremely trashing site your detector may be resetting it's threshold just as it passes over that very old liberty seated dime at six inches. This just might cause you to miss the next "good" target.

When adjusting this feature remember that stability is most important. Never set your SAT speed to the point where chatter and confusing responses interferes with your ability to hear and to analyze. Typical or normal coin searching usually requires slower speeds, while trashy sites, beach hunting and relic hunting sometimes demand faster speeds (higher numbers).

THE SEARCHCOIL

Searchcoils, no matter what their configuration (co-planar, co-axial, 2D, etc.) are all pretty comparable in regards to efficiency. Your ability to detect deep, for the most part, comes from the detector's circuitry, the use of optimum settings, and your experience and expertise. Certainly the size of the coil matters when it comes to the matrix it can produce, but comparing an eight inch searchcoil from one manufacturer to the eight inch coil of another is time wasted. Each manufacturer's engineering departments design their searchcoils to function with their models and their features.

The Spectrum 9 1/2 inch coil is my workhorse, and I use it probably 80% of the time in the field!

If you are serious about coinhunting you will have in your arsenal a small sniper coil, a standard 8 to 9 inch coil and a deepseeking 12 to 14 inch coil. Each has its purpose, and knowing when to use them and why is important!

The standard eight or nine inch searchcoil is your workhorse, and will suffice for 80% of your coinhunting. It's small enough not to be bothered by a lot of trash, yet big enough to give reasonable depth. This will be the coil of record if you will, and will be responsible for most all of your coin finds.

The small coil or "sniper", as it's typically called is very often the "only coil" for the trashy site. It's downward matrix is narrow, and perfect for probing between the junk items present. It can "sneak" down to that old dime hiding to the left of the pull tab, and it can isolate that old liberty quarter, that for so long was masqueraded by the bottlecap next to it. It's designed for delicate searching, and it's worth its weight in gold. Using a sniper coil can be tedious, and will certainly slow your search, but it's definitely worth the effort.

The oversize or "deepseeking" coil (typically anywhere from 12 to 15 inches) will take you to depths unknown. As you might expect the larger a coil....the deeper it goes. As would also be expected....the larger the coil..... the more it sees! As a result it is not suited for use in an area that is laden with a lot of trash. If used in this circumstance it will merely sound off over and over again, reacting to the many trash items it is seeing. Better to opt for the small sniper coil, and isolate the good from the bad. Use this deepseeking coil in minimal target areas, or those considered hunted out. Use it in conjuction with the all metal mode and it will put you down where the devil and the good ones are hiding!

Each coil has a purpose, and each site will dictate which you should consider. Many detectorists I know never consider the smaller sniper coil, and this amazes me. To me, next to the standard eight inch, it's the most versatile and the most productive of the group. Yes I move along at a snail's pace, but what do I care as long as older coins are coming to the surface?

Bottom line: <u>Use the standard eight or nine inch coil under typical conditions. Use the small sniper coil in enclosed, narrow areas, and sites laden with trash. Use the larger deepseeking coil in relatively clean, and typically hunted out sites.</u>

HEADPHONES

No matter how expensive or sophisticated your metal detector is you must use a good set of headphones if you are to become adept at finding the deeper coins. Using the detector's speaker system solely will <u>not</u> work! At best you will only hear the large and shallow items, and most likely miss coins from about four inches on down. Aside from the limited audio output the detector has outside noise from traffic, crowds or wind will add to this problem.

You do not have to spend a great deal of money on headphones....simply don't buy the least expensive, or the most expensive. Headphones in the $50 to $100 range will suffice quite nicely, but be sure they have individual volume controls. You may not think that you have hearing problems, but quite frequently one ear is less sensitive and having individual volume controls will allow you to adjust accordingly. <u>Set your detectors volume as loud as possible, then adjust the volume controls on your headphones.</u>

COMPUTERIZED METAL DETECTORS

Over the past 25 years I've used almost every brand and model of metal detector available, and let me assure you....the computerized metal detector is here to stay! Technological advancements and inroads have convinced me that my coinshooting can only get better. It stands to reason that if a computer programmer can understand my goals, and the physical obstacles I face, my equipment will continue to improve rapidly over the coming years.

Critical, sensitive control adjustments made by the user a few years ago are now handled automatically by a detector's computerized circuitry, leaving today's coin hunter to concentrate on the more important aspects of the search itself. Ground balancing, tuning and threshold are quickly and automatically dealt with and almost seem to operate on their own. The negative side of all this is that we've become more dependent...more prone to assumptions. We must constantly remind ourselves that computers will only do what they have been programmed to do. Likewise we must be able to read between the advertising hype, never believing 100% of what we read. Ultimately what determines our success in the field will be knowing when to add a dash of experience, a little common sense, and a dab of intuition......a formula that has always worked well in almost every area!

> "It stands to reason if a computer programmer can understand our goals, and the physical obstacles we face, the equipment will continue to improve rapidly over the coming years."

THE BEST DETECTOR AVAILABLE

I have often been asked what is the best metal detector on the market. Is there one that I would recommend? It's not an easy question to answer, and it's a topic that can be bantered about, debated and argued. Ask ten detectorists and you will likely receive ten different responses. At present I am using the White's Spectrum XLT. Why? Because as of now it offers me every possible advantage I need to find the older and deeper coins. I can fine tune each feature to the umpteenth degree, and gain that inch or two that puts me ahead of the competition. Does that mean I

The Spectrum XLT has become my buddy, my right hand, and the best deep coin finder on the block!

endorse this product? As of now yes! Next year? I don't know. I will say however that White's Electronics has consistently been first with those features that improve my odds such as VLF, the target ID meter, and the Eagle was the first computerized detector, even if others boast of having the first "patented" model. They also were the first to offer signal balance, which I like a great deal, and the first to offer target signature readouts (Spectrum), an extremely valuable tool for accurate identification of targets.

Features, options and manufacturer claims will come and go in this industry, and it's important to understand what is real and what is hype. Do we need a detector that will go an inch or two deeper. Yes! Do we need a detector that talks to us? I don't think so. Do we need a detector that is built to withstand in the field use and accidental abuse? Yes. An inch or two more depth, dependability, smooth performance and proven results are what matters to the hobbyist, and the detector that offers all this is the best detector on the market. For me, at this time, it's the Spectrum XLT!

RECOVERY TOOLS

To properly recover coins you will need a few different digging tools. First you will need a sharp trowel. One with a long and durable blade. One that will not bend with hard soil, and one that will offer leverage. Keep it honed at all times.

Next have a good probe. This is probably the most important recovery vehicle you have. When used properly it will allow you to detect the most manicured grounds around. Probing not only leaves the ground in good stead...it also minimizes damage to potentially valuable coins. Probing for coins is a skill that can be learned quickly and one that you will utilize often.

YOUR OWN PRACTICE SITE

To better understand your metal detector, it's functions and operating characteristics, design a practice area in your backyard or somewhere on your property. It does not have to be elaborate ....merely an area where you can be sure your detector is not only working correctly, but that it's working to the max. The area should be at least twenty five feet by five feet in size, and should contain coins, jewelry, trash and anything else you might encounter in the field.

Use most all the denominations of coins, and while you are not interested in finding trash items, be sure to include them so you will understand your detector's reaction to them, as well as it's ability to reject them. Write down the location and depth of each item you bury (you will remember initially but forget later).

How you design your practice area is entirely up to you. Be realistic however; do not bury items at excessive depths, and at the same time keep in mind your objective....those coins just out of reach of the competition. I suggest you bury your targets anywhere from three to ten inches deep (the latter depth is the area where you must excel).

Have a small section where you you can practice isolating good from bad. Place coins in close proximity to bottlecaps, and pulltabs, and place a few above and beneath. This will be a good area to practice using your small sniper coil, and in the process help you better understand how to decipher those erratic, and very confusing signals you encounter in the field.

Once you've completed your practice area begin scanning your coil over the various items you buried. Listen closely to how your detector responds, and if you have target ID display, note their readouts. Experiment with your discrimination. Know exactly each metallic rejection setting (your discrimination controls may be labeled, but every detector is somewhat different), and rejection points may vary slightly from the factory presets).

Listen carefully how your detector responds to each item. Try and discern their tell-tale audio responses, and make mental notes of what you might expect when encountering them in the field.

Some items will sound somewhat alike, but many will offer characteristic responses allowing you to predermine what the target is before you recover it.

IN THE FIELD CONSIDERATIONS

Now that you know more about your metal detector's controls and capabilities let's talk about putting this knowledge to use to find those deep, older and more often than not, more valuable, coins. First consider the baseball manager who says "we're going back to the basics to win ballgames. We'll learn to bunt, field and do all that's necessary to become a competitive and sound club!" Well this also applies to you as well....know the settings that allow your detector to work more efficiently, never forget the basic technics of operating a metal detector, and perform accordingly! Taking shortcuts or the easy way out will always work against you. You will come home with a handful of coins....clad and worth face value!

Much of what follows may seem redundant, but I don't care. Proper and adequate search techniques are important if you are to ever gain any advantage over the average TH'er. I assure you that no matter how much you "think" you know you will often overlook the basic, golden rules of

> *"Proper and adequate search techniques are important if you are to ever gain any advantage over the average TH'er."*

metal detecting, and yes, after twenty years of detecting, I still have to remind myself of them as well.

SCANNING YOUR COIL

First of my nagging recommendations.... <u>ALWAYS KEEP YOUR COIL CLOSE TO THE GROUND, AND ALWAYS OVERLAP YOUR SWEEPS BY AT LEAST ONE THIRD!</u> Forget one half.....overlap by one third!! You will feel like you are moving at a snails pace, and that's because you are! Get used to it! This is your new, "deep coin" scanning speed! Even before I overlapped by one third I thought I was moving slow, but after slowing down more my returns improved dramatically. I cannot emphasize enough...slow down, and slow down again. You are <u>not</u> covering the ground adequately enough, no matter what you may think!

One mechanical method I use to insure adequate ground coverage is shortening my detector's stem so that the coil is literally at my feet. Full extension puts it too far in front of me, making my swings erratic and haphazard. Shortening it corrects this problem, and actually hinders any notions you have to scan quickly. Keep your searchcoil close to the ground, and keep it parallel. Why? Because you need every inch....every advantage. Most detectorists become bored, and as a result start scanning haphazardly, dishing the coil, leaving valuable treasures behind. Focus on your goal, your plan for the day, and keep your coil parellel to the ground. Remember the basics....you will come home a winner!

SIGNALS...TREASURE OR TRASH?

No matter what site or area you metal detect you will receive signals. Some obviously good, some obviously bad, and others confusing and difficult to decipher! Unusual? Not at all! Cause for concern? Not really! All the signals you receive, no matter how undistinguishable, have some characteristic response. Learning them will take time, and there will always be a few you don't comprehend.....these must be dug! Blips, bongs, scratches, and bangs, no matter the sound, all mean something, and it's up to you to label them. When you started out metal detecting you probably dug most every response you received in order to better understand your machine. Without knowing it you fine tuned your hearing, and as a result you are better equipped now to define those responses. Trust in your experience, and your intuition to determine which signals are good and which are bad. The final thought I will leave you with, and one that guides me each time out...."when in doubt dig!"

> *"ONE REASON EXPERIENCE IS SUCH*
> *A GOOD TEACHER*
> *IS THAT SHE DOESN'T ALLOW ANY DROPOUTS"*

SITE CHARACTERISTICS

Just like you recognize an old face you will eventually begin to recognize those areas that offer good detecting. You will have that intuition, that sixth sense, that says <u>this is it!</u> You will recognize clues, and you will begin gaining confidence in your ability to analyze. Old areas look old and recognizing them gets easier as you continue to spend time in the field.

An area that is old will often have vegetation (shrubs, flowers or plants) foreign to the surrounding area. You might call them human embellishments. They are visually obvious, and an instant indication that the site was inhabited at some time and worth searching. It's very easy to see these things, but it's up to you to look for them.

Trees will often tell you a great deal about a site, but only if you know what to look for. A cluster of trees in a open area may

This spreading and very foreign cactus plant was the clue that I had found the old homesite I was searching for.

indicate what was a windbreak or shade-provider for a home years ago. Many times the trees will be all that remains. You should also be able to identify trees, or at least the major categories, and know which are indicative of older habitation. For instance the average lifespan of a Willow or Sycamore tree is under 25 years, whereas Oaks and Magnolias have a long lifespan well over 50 years. Facts like this are not always dependable but certainly helpful when trying to ascertain the age of an area.

If the site you are considering happens to be an open area or field do a little reconnaissance before you start your search. Look for any indication of prior use or habitation. Does it appear it's an area that has been tended to or plowed in the past? What telltale clues are present? Can you identify pieces of glass or oyster shells, broken brick, pottery or perhaps scraps of wood? Be alert for any clues that would indicate the area was inhabited or used by human beings. They will offer you a starting point for your search, a better idea of what the site was like years ago, and certainly a more positive outlook for your day.

The ground itself will also give clues as to whether the area is old or new. The soil might be heavily compacted, rough in texture, and very uneven....the result of traffic and use. More soil than turf, and a varied mixture of grasses and weeds. Old ground will also typically hold more trash. Why? Because it is an area that was "used", and while it would be nice if those who used it only lost coins, that didn't happen! Concentrations of signals, good or bad, are indicative of an area that is or was used, and worthy of investigation. On the flip side an area that produces absolutely no signals is more than likely virgin or unworthy of follow-up.

One last comment about any potential site. Does it look like an area that was used? If that sounds somewhat silly it's not. Use a little intuition and study an area. Does it look like it might have been used for a picnic, or is it ideal for holding a carnival or other large happening. Is it an area that offers shade in the summer, and is it's ground vegetation somewhat low? Is it readily accessible from a road? Is there evidence of an entrance or of heavy traffic? Try to "get a feel" for an area.....if you yourself feel comfortable in it that just maybe the answer you are looking for.

THE FIRST SEARCH OF A SITE

The first visit to an area is distinctly different from the second, third, fourth or fifth. It demands a "getting acquainted" search. One where you grope for clues or indications that the area you are in is the correct one, and more important, deserving of further time and effort.

> "Ground mineralization, vegetation, temperature, humidity, the amount of use the site has seen, and the type of trash present are all factors that must be considered when deciding on an approach."

It can also be an exciting search as well if you happen to be the first detectorist to search it. You always research hoping for a prime site, and when everything works just right you will never forget it!!

Remember that no two sites are alike, and each demands a different approach. Ground mineralization, vegetation, temperature/humidity, the amount of use the site has seen, and the amount and type of trash present are all factors that must be considered when deciding on an approach. You can began searching with preset indicators, but remember what I said earlier....average settings produce average results.

The best way to gauge any new site quickly is to start scanning in the all-metal mode.

The best way to gauge any new area is to start searching in the all metal mode. By using this mode you will learn how much mineralization is present, and what specific adjustments will need to be made. Erratic threshold or drift resulting from heavy mineralization can be corrected by manually ground balancing your detector. Once you do this began digging every signal to get an accurate picture of what you will have to contend with. Are there one or two particular trash items that predominate the area? If so, what are they, and what will it take to eliminate them and still find your deeper coins? Are these items scattered randomly or do they proliferate the area? Will you be able to search the site easily, or will you have to remove a great deal of the trash to have a chance at what's below?

Now you might say this type of analyzation is a lot of work, but stopping to think over your situation can save you a great deal of time and a lot of frustration. The tendency most detectorists have is to jump in head first, search haphazardly, get frustrated and then decide the area's not worth the time and effort. If you've researched the site and it has potential it's worth the time and effort!! Like anything else in life nothing is insurmountable, and taking a few minutes to decide on a plan of action will almost always work wonders. I am certainly not implying that by analyzing each site your searching will be a piece of cake, but I am certain it will make your job easier.

There may be times when you find an area that has long term potential. In other words the best it has to offer will take time. It could be the amount of trash present or it might be that mineralization is heavy and varies within the area. It might be that the site is in close proximity to high tension towers or some other outside influence that will affect your search. Perhaps the targets are at a depth where they are only audible when the soil is saturated, such as after a heavy rain. It could also be available to you only at specific times of the year (for instance a boy scout camp during off season).

Whatever the reasons never give up on a site you feel good about. Intuition is a valuable asset, and letting it guide you can very often make the difference in a good day or bad day. I remember coming up empty at a few sites, but down deep knew that there had to be "something" there. My "gut feelings" more often than not were correct, and often it was a matter of finding that one hotspot with the area itself, or using a different approach.

Proper research, good site analyzation, decent equipment,

and a little intuition are generally all you will need to be successful at any site. Always remember however that you will not find coins where none were lost! If you are in the wrong place the best equipment in the world and the amazing Kreskin won't help!

"PATIENCE IS THE ART OF CONCEALING YOUR IMPATIENCE"

"Whatever the reasons never give up on a site you feel good about. Intuition is a valuable asset, and letting it guide you can very often make the difference in a good day or bad day!"

GROUND MINERALIZATION

Ground mineralization can be a big factor when determining how well you will do in a given area, and it is a term that is confusing, and very much misunderstood. Years ago mineralization was actually easier to explain since many of the advancements we have today were not available, and erratic operation was obvious. Today's technology compensates, tends to hide the problem, and as a result makes it's difficult for the detectorist to know when he or she is in an area of heavy mineralization!

What is mineralization? What happens when you encounter it, and what can you expect to hear or find? First off you know best how your metal detector typically works or operates. If you happen to be searching a site and it's acting erratically or differently chances are you've encountered ground mineralization. One way you might determine this..... drag a magnet through the soil and see if it picks up a small particles of iron or mineralized fuzz. Another more routine method is to analyze the targets you recover in the area. If mineralization is heavy, coins, especially copper ones, will be pitted or heavily corroded (Silver coins may also be affected but not to the extent copper and brass objects are)!

You might also switch over to your all metal mode of operation, and began scanning. If your threshold is overly touchy or erratic you've encountered mineralization. How to overcome this problem? Simply.....manually ground balance in the all metal mode!

Automatic ground balancing has it's merits, especially given the manipulations and adjustments that are associated with the manual method. It allows the user to spend more time hunting and less time turning knobs. The drawback of course is that it glosses over the mineralization problem, offers only an averaging, and provides the user with a false sense of security. Yes your detector will be humming along with little if any chatter but it will be limited in it's ability to punch down and through to where the older, more valuable coins are. The serious prospector always manually ground balances his detector, and when possible does so with a ten turn tuner or pot. Why? Because it allows for extremely fine tuning or as I like to say "a little finesse", something necessary when you are faced with an exact and difficult challenge. Fine tuning anything makes it work better, and getting rid of mineralization by manually ground balancing your detector will make it more efficient when searching for coins. That extra fine edge that the prospector gets will work for you as well, and put you ahead of the average hunter. If you can relate to a radio station that is "tuned in" you will understand the theory behind fine tuning your detector, and having it work to the "max"!

When you manually ground balance do it slowly and be as precise as possible. Listen closely to your audio, both at waist and ground level throughout your searching, adjusting accordingly. It can mean the difference between valuable coins and "run of the mill" finds. Keep your coil at one constant height throughout your search, to avoid backreading and overshoot signals.

SEARCHING MONEY SITES

Quite often you will need to make quick decisions about where to spend your time detecting. You may only have an hour or two to get out and enjoy your pastime, and you will need to choose your site wisely. What do you do? No problem....choose a "money site". A money site is any site that offers the best return on your time. It's an area that tends to give up more because those who used it or went there had to have money. Such as? Well for starters how about carnival grounds, circus sites, athletic fields, roadside vendors, admission areas to outdoor drive ins....? There are others, but to complete the list you have to ask yourself if money was needed? If it was, it was surely lost, making that site the best one available for a limited amount of time. The more money that was carried, the more that was lost, and the better your odds................

THOSE HUNTED OUT SPOTS

We've all heard about sites that were "cleaned out" by other detectorists. Hunted to death....absolutely nothing left to find...null and void! If you are any kind of coin hunter you know this is balderdash. I have yet to find one site that was hunted out. Sparse perhaps, but never void of a few good coins. In fact when I hear such comments the site become a challenge for me. Tell me I'm wasting my time and I'll go to work to prove you wrong. Why? Well let me explain a little further....

First, "hunted out" sites are not easy pickings. They are difficult areas to search, but very often they are worth the extra effort. When approaching such an area assume that anyone searching it will <u>not</u> hear many signals because those that hunted it before cleaned out the trash, and went home with the newer surface coins. That eliminates one problem. The other possibility of course is that the site may have been so trashy that those before you did not remove the junk, and came home with what their detectors could easily distinguish, leaving behind a great many coins for the patient hunter. Typically however the first scenario is the correct one....an area seemingly is void of any signals whatsoever.

When you encounter such an area stop and consider the following:

- Did everyone who hunted the site utilize their larger coil?
- Did they search in a silent mode of operation?
- Did they hunt exclusively in the discriminate mode?
- Did they have the latest in detector technology?
- Did they know how to use their detectors to the max?
- Were they patient and careful in their searching.
- Were they careful to overlap their sweeps by one third?
- Did they check fringe areas or perimeters of the site?
- Were they really listening for the "whispers" that only the very deep coins offer?
- Did they grid areas to ensure adequate coverage?
- Did they hunt the site after a good rain?
- Did they increase their sensitivity to the max, or search in the all metal mode?
- Did they ever consider digging the marginal signals (those mid-range meter readings?

After you've considered all of these valid questions develop a plan of action. First do a quick search to ascertain what the site offers in the way of signals. Next tell yourself that the secret to conquering the area will be patience. Understand that you will be moving at a snails pace, listening for faint whispers of very deep coins. Accept that fact that you will be hunting with audio threshold.....just perhaps turned up just a notch. Know that any type of faint meter movement, coupled with a variance in audio might be the <u>only</u> clue you will receive. Know that "thoroughly" searching the site might take days, not hours, and then decide exactly what plot of ground you will be hunting first.

After you've decided on your plan of attack adjust the controls on your detector so that it's operating at it's maximum level. Increase depth or sensitivity as far as possible (just prior to chatter or erratic operation). If the site is clean, and your detector has a recovery adjustment set it for slow. This might sound detrimental but it is not..... a slower recovery rate will actually work better on deeper coins! Set your discrimination to a notch below nickel acceptance, and turn your threshold up a notch. Threshold should be a constant drone in your headset if you are to hear any minor inflection, especially in an area of heavy traffic or outside noise.

If you are able to control the "target volume" (not threshold volume) do so, and turn it all the way up. Then set the volume controls on your headset so that the threshold is not overpowering but just barely audible. Then shorten the detectors stem or rod so that the searchcoil literally winds up at your feet. This will force you to scan at a slower rate, insuring better ground coverage. Having the coil out in front makes it difficult to adequately cover the ground. With it in this position you can better judge one third overlaps.

Remember too when hunting such a site that you will in all likelihood have to walk directly over that old coin in order to find it. Don't always depend on fringe detection to do it for you. You will need to be lucky, and you will also need to be adept and patient. Remember the hardware you have at your disposal and utilize it. Draw on your experience and expertise, and you will be successful where others have failed! The coins you seek are deep, the signals barely discernable, but the rewards are worth your concentration and effort.

RECOVERING COINS

Once you receive that positive or good signal, how do you go about recovering the target.....the coin? Exactly how are you going to bring it to the surface? Recovering the coins you find is almost as important as finding them. Careless or haphazard

Always recover any coin slowly and deliberately . . . . being sure not to disturb the area you are hunting.

recovery can ruin a day's work and a month's worth of research. Knowing coins are in the ground is the first step....actually putting them in your pouch is next.

If you are a professional and/or a serious coinhunter you will utilize a <u>probe</u>. A probe is a long "ice pick" type of tool, and with it you probe the ground, and ascertain exactly where the coin or the target really is. It will allow you to physically touch the coin before you recover it, and sometimes tell you the best way to recover it. Once you've come into contact the target back off, make a vertical slice in the turf, keeping the point of the probe stationary. Then, do the same thing horizontally. This will leave you with an "X" in the turf, and your target in the middle. Insert the probe under the target, and pry it to the surface, being careful of course not to scratch it in the process. After retrieving it push the folds of the turf together, step on the spot and continue your search....! Sound easy? It's not, but with a little practice it can become second nature with you, and put you in a class far above those who merely care to plow staight ahead!

IDEAS & TECHNIQUES FOR EACH TYPE OF SITE

Over the years I learned a great many things that enabled me to a better coin hunter. As I stated earlier most of it the result of trial and error; some of it accidental! This learning process made each successive outing more productive, allowing me to find more older coins in less time. In this chapter I'd like to share a few experiences, a few ideas and a few techniques as they relate to the various sites. Hopefully they will help you when in the field. They should work to your advantage.

Before we begin, let me remind you that proper and adequate search techniques must be employed throughout any search. No matter what ideas or strategies you might gain from reading this book, without thorough and careful search techniques you're wasting your time!! Move slowly, overlap your sweeps, keep you searchcoil parallel, and know when to make physical changes so that your detector will <u>always</u> be working to the max! Be consistent, be thorough and you will succeed!

> "No matter what ideas or strategies you might gain from reading this book, without thorough and careful search techniques you're wasting our time."

Dick Stout

"COMMON SENSE IS
THE KNACK OF SEEING THINGS AS THEY ARE, AND
DOING THINGS AS THEY OUGHT TO BE DONE"

THE BEST COIN SITE

Every detectorist has his or her favorite site. Some like old schools, while others favor city parks, and there are those whoo seek out old homesites or swimming areas. Frankly it depends upon your locale and your past experiences. The site <u>YOU</u> like best will be the one where <u>YOU</u> found the best and/or oldest finds. My favorite site?   <u>The old rural picnic grove!</u>   Why? Because they are plentiful, always overlooked by the average treasure hunter, and they inevitably give up a lot of old coins. If you happen to be the first to search an old grove you will understand why I am partial to this area.

RURAL PICNIC GROVES

The key word is <u>grove</u>! Today we have picnic "areas" or picnic "grounds". Many years ago we congregated at the <u>grove</u>! Everyone knew where it was, and used it. It was not unusual for the people in the area to be at the grove on the weekend to escape the heat of summer, and to visit with others in the community. They brought picnic baskets, sometimes bathing suits and they socialized hours on end. It was <u>the</u> place to be and often <u>the</u> place to be seen. Do something frivolous or risque, and the whole town knew about it on Monday! That's how important this area was at the turn of the century!

Eventually radio, theaters and television came along, and the grove became less popular. What was once a community meeting place disappeared.... out of sight...out of mind.....one reason it's proven to be such a plus for the coin shooter of today. This site today is often just a grove of trees, camouflaged over the years by mother nature, and waiting to be discovered by the dedicated coinhunter.

Old groves were often named after the landowner or a land-mark. Names like Johnson's Grove, Smith's grove, Elm Grove and Oak Grove were common, and because the area attracted a lot of people quite often the landowner set up a concession stand, selling soda pop, and snack food.....taking advantage of the rules of supply and demand.

FINDING A GROVE

How do you find an old picnic grove? Well, first you must know what to look for! Aside from keying on the "grove" roads and streets in your neighborhood, learn to recognize the telltale clues this site will offer....

First know that the grove was never too far from town. It almost always had large trees to provide shade, quite often a creek or stream, and minimal ground vegetation. It also was accessible from the main road via a driveway or lane, and sometimes offered an area where cars or horse drawn buggies could be left. (This entrance may be not be obvious today.......look carefully for a filled in ditch). There might also be an open area or field immediately adjacent for games and/or sporting events.

When you think you've found an old grove area walk it, look for worn paths and indications of past use. Look for old structures, rusty bottlecaps, square nails, oyster shells or small pieces of glass, and finally ask yourself if it looks like the kind of place you would take your family for a picnic? Let your intuition come into play, and proceed from there. Your impressions of an area or "gut reactions" are often good ones.....act on them!

You'll often find documentation of the local grove in a community's history book, church records or in an old newspaper. You might learn about the area from an older senior citizen who went there years ago, or you might see it in an old photograph

The roots of this big tree gave up five old coins in New Jersey . . . .
it was in an old picnic grove used in the late 1800's!

found in an attic. Almost all small communities had such an area.....the chances are very good it still looks like it did years ago, and if you are the first to detect it, you are in for a treat.

MY FIRST GROVE

I'll always remember finding, and searching my first grove.... interesting how I found it, exciting when I searched it, and one of the best learning experiences I've had as a coinhunter......

My metal detecting buddy Dan Hamilton, and I were members of a local historical society in Hunterdon County, New Jersey, and at one of the monthly meetings an individual mentioned an old thoroughfare called "picnic grove" road. Instantly we were saying "hold on a minute..whoa"..back up a second!!" What, when and where? We had lived in the township for some time, but had never heard of picnic grove road?

We quickly learned that this road was now nothing more than an overgrown path off one of the back roads in the township, but at the turn of the century was the hub of the area's social life. It lead to (what else) the town grove! We learned all we could about the site at this meeting. As you can imagine we couldn't wait to detect it! A couple days later we found the road, and what we surmised was the grove. We wanted to start searching then and there; instead we went to the county tax office to find the owner of the property. We discovered he lived almost sixty miles away in northern New Jersey, and after a phone call, a polite request to hunt, we were back on the site ready to recover it's treasures.

The long and short of it is that Dan and I spent close to six months working the grove, finding hundreds of old coins..... nothing newer than 1910! Indian Head cents, Shield and Barber nickels, Liberty Seated and Barber dimes, Barber quarters, halves and lots of old and very valuable jewelry items. Sound too good to be true....well it was! It was an exciting time and a very profitable site.

The thrill of searching this grove, and finding one old coin after another was something neither Dan nor I had experienced before. We felt certain we were the first to find this site, and the first ones to detect it. We also knew that we had to find more just like it. Any meter reading in the plus range of our ID meters was silver, with Indian Head pennies registering just below penny, and best of all we were not hampered by today's trash. We were also lucky to have peace and quiet, and a beautiful setting for our searches of the area....a real paradise to say the least!

After this we began looking for other groves in our area. Based on what the first looked like it was not hard to start noticing others, or at least what we surmised were others. We drove the back roads, talked to a lot of people, and spent a great deal of time at the tax office finding out who owned these potentially rewarding sites. We sometimes found that the landowners knew the history of their property, and could confirm our hunches. Others simply did not know, or were too new to the area. In those cases we asked permission to search, and were usually given permission.

> "Dan and I spent close to six months working the grove, literally finding hundreds of old coins . . . . nothing newer than 1910!"

Another reason I consider the picnic grove the best coin hunting site is that it's not difficult to get permission to search it. It's a wooded area, and one that would <u>not</u> be greatly affected by someone digging coin size targets. I also knew that the other coinhunters in the area were hunting the typical sites...the school grounds, the parks, the ballfields, but <u>NOT</u> the camouflaged, and forgotten grove areas that I had found.... <u>Advantage....ME!!</u>

SEARCHING THE PICNIC GROVE

When you detect an old picnic grove for the first time set your detector to all-metal, and dig all signals. You typically won't have a lot of trash, and digging all of your signals will prove helpful by alerting you to the signals of other potentially valuable items like jewelry and keepsakes. Remember that many of the items you find at an old, old grove are not your routine finds? They are old and have been in the ground sometime. Learn them and where they fall on your meter!

In the old groves I've searched, coins seemed to be everywhere. In creek beds, on their banks, under tree roots and in and around trash pits. From my perspective those who used the grove had no particular patterns or habits. If you find a hot spot work it, and work your way outward. I also found that after many trips to these sites I could go back and search perimeters, lanes, around the bases of trees and still find more. It was also not unusual to find coins among the shrubs since many grew after the grove was abandoned.

This obscure path was once a road in the late 1800's . . . . leading to an old grove used for church gatherings.

If the grove has a small creek or stream search the creekbed itself, and look for that one particular area that might have been the proverbial "swimming hole". This is not always a sure thing but it's certainly a possibility! There were also a few groves that I searched that had small buildings standing, and/or indications that they existed at one time or another. I guessed that they were concession stands or cabins used for bathers to change clothes? If they're not now an obvious landmark an abundance of square nails or construction materials will usually indicate where they once stood. Old picnic groves are profitable, not that difficult to find, and simply waiting for you to discover them. Get busy and find out why I consider them my favorite coin site!

CITY PARKS

The term "city" park is really not definitive. They are not all alike, and in fact differ considerably. The City Park might be that large recreational area within a very large city.... or it might be the town square in the rural New England community. It could also be that large, sprawling acreage on the edge of town that is used for picnicking, baseball, football and swimming. They are all very different, yet still defined city parks. I have searched them, in particular the old ones, and no two are alike.

Large cities like New York have "large" parks like Central Park, and they are a breed unto themselves. They are not only large, and extremely old, but extremely good for finding valuable coins. They also demand a different plan of action and a different approach. They are so large that you must research them much as you would a small community. You must find out which section of the park came first, how it was designed and enlarged over the years, what activities took place, and what areas should be avoided.

Large city parks offer recreational areas and facilities, swimming pools, band shells, jogging trails and bridle paths and picnic areas. They have boccie ball areas, horseshoe pits, game tables (chess), flower gardens and sometimes zoos. They have sprawling grassy areas for spreading blankets, and for listening to concerts, speeches, and for holding hands. They are frequently the oasis within the jungle and as a result provide excellent detecting.

Because of their age, large city parks have been used by thousands, if not millions of people over the years, but you will still have better luck searching these areas if you research them, and talk to people who know their history. Potluck searching, with a few decent finds is possible, but not recommended....it can also be extremely dangerous! Your first consideration in any of these areas should be that of personal safety. <u>Always, and I mean always, search with a companion.</u> Stay within sight of one an-other, and have signals so that you can alert each other to poten-tial danger. Crime today is an unfortunate aspect of big city life, but it's real, and something we must be aware of. Ignorance can get you into a lot of trouble quickly.

SEARCHING LARGE PARKS

Searching a large city park can be an awesome task, and knowing where to start is difficult. You will likely have some preliminary information to go on before you visit the site, but if you do not, start your search in the obvious places......the band shell area, along the walking paths and around benches, along the banks of the lake or pond or the grassy strip around the pool. Remember the playground area, the ballfield, the picnic areas and the obvious routes from one point to another (usually worn and obvious to the eye).

When coinshooting this site be prepared for a lot of trash and a few good finds interspersed. These infrequent goodies are worth the effort. Go slow, overlap by at least one third, consider using your sniper coil, and if necessary lower your sensitivity. Concen-trate on separating the good from the bad... and remember old city parks offer old coins! Patience will definitely be a virtue!

You'll also find old coins at shallow depths in large city parks because the average detector users were lazy, and did not want to dig a lot of trash, or because they assumed nothing old could be that close to the surface. Never ignore loud signals in a large city park. More often than not you will surprise yourself!! I've found more valuable coins at noticeably shallower depths in city parks than at any other site I've detected.

When you search this type of area always consider the improbable or least likely. Place your searchcoil in the middle of a bush, under that rock or give it a try in the heavy overgrowth that borders or surrounds the park. I am not sure why these difficult areas produce so many coins but they frequently do. I can only guess that vegetation began "creeping in", obscuring what used to be useable space. It's also a possibility that the "average" detectorist was not that dedicated or professional enough to do the same thing. Remember that guy... the average detectorist....he's everywhere and nowhere at the same time!

> *"You'll often find very old, valuable coins at shallow depths in large city parks because other TH'ers were lazy, and did not want to hassle the trash, or because they assumed nothing old could be that close to the surface."*

SMALL TOWN PARKS

If you detect smaller community parks or squares you will find older coins, but obviously not the quantities that you will find in the larger city park. As you also might expect you should look at these sites quite differently! The smaller town square is an integral part of almost every small community in the country, espe-

Many old coins are found at very shallow depths in old parks simply because other detectorists assumed their responses were too loud to be anything other than surface trash.

cially in the southern states and in New England. They are small, quaint, picturesque and productive coin sites because many detectorists "assume" they can't hunt them, or because they are self-conscious about being seen in such a setting.

The fact is......not many people in these smaller communities notice or care whether you are detecting their park. Yes you're using a metal detector...so what? They typically could care less! What am I trying to say? <u>Nothing ventured, nothing gained...get up some courage.</u> If you are worried about ordinances or regulations and none are posted, ask at the police station. You'll be surprised when they give you the go ahead. Search the town square, have fun, and be sure to use a probe.

SEARCHING THE TOWN SQUARE

Frankly there are no definitive techniques for searching smaller parks. I'll usually start around the bandshell or gazebo (if there is one), and work my way outward. Search around benches, paths, and grassy strips between the sidewalk and the street (again an area that is frequently overlooked).

Next work the entrances to the square, and then concentrate on those spots that offer the greatest benefits to those using the area....the shady areas, those close to the bandstand and those closest to the concession stand or fountain.

These old coins were recovered in a very small town square in Northeast Texas.

The smaller, town square will have "some" trash, but for the most part they will offer trouble free searching. The signals may not be frequent, but those that you do receive are worthy of followup, especially the faint ones. Almost all the small town parks I searched gave up fewer coins, but those that did turn up were usually older and more valuable. I attribute this to the fact that others hunted the site, took the easiest and most obvious, and left the best for those who worked just a little harder!

If the area is relatively free of garbage, hunt in the all-metal mode and double check in disc. Remember that most of the lightweight or shallow coins were more than likely found already. You are going for the old and the deep. Adjust accordingly, and be patient. As I said before, listen for the faint signal, the subtle signal, the <u>whisper</u>......it's <u>THE COIN</u> you are after!! The one that those who searched before you didn't take the time to notice!

Work a very small area, and search it again.....know that when you are through that section is clean and has nothing to offer....period!! Last but not least always keep in mind the age of the site, the potential, and the ramifications of a haphazard search of the area.

OLD SCHOOLS

Keyword..............OLD!!

Schools are everywhere......<u>old ones are not!</u> In the same breath I must tell you that old schools are not that difficult to find....those that are able to provide old and valuable coins are! By that I mean that the most accessible, and the easiest to re-search school site has already been hunted. Always give the competition credit and search for those that they tired of looking for.

Old schools can be found in large metropolitan areas, and in rural, countryside settings. They may still be in use or else trans-formed into residences. They might also be non-existent, or shells of what they used to be. Whatever their current status or condition it behooves you to find them and search them.

What exactly is an "old" school? It might be debateable, but to me an old school is one that was in use before 1940. I realize that may not seem old to many, but it's a site that was active before I was born...and maybe that's not a good benchmark, but it's one that I accept. What's really important is the date the site was first used. It might have been abandoned in 1940, but if it was first in use in 1900 that offers 40 years of finds. If in fact it was first in use in 1938 that lessens the probabilities. Good research will answer these questions!

This old one room school in rural New Jersey was completely camouflaged in the summertime . . . . making any searching extremely difficult.

Older, rural schools were often small, one room structures. Because of this their enrollment was usually small, and this alone will lessen the total number of coins you might find. Not the quality...but the numbers!! Remember too if the school was in use for many years your "quantity odds" increase. Another factor to consider is whether or not you are the first to be hunting the area....if so your "keepers" will certainly be good.

When searching these sites be congizant of the fact that kids who went to school in the late 1800's or early 1900's did not have a lot of money, and as a result did not bring it to school. Back then a nickel went a lot further, and the more affluent usually attended private schools (another area to consider?). Meals were usually packed and brought in, and the number of days when any money was needed were few and far between. Certainly a few coins were lost, but not large denominations, and certainly not in great numbers. Your ace in the hole once again....long, long term use of the school and site!

*"SCHOOL IS THE MOUSE RACE THAT
EQUIPS YOU FOR THE RAT RACE"*

SEARCHING OLD SCHOOL SITES

When you search an old school site the size of the school itself will play a part in your search. Rural one room schools will obviously not provide you with the number of coins that a larger institution will, but not all schools before the turn of the century were one room. What importance does this have on your search? Simply that you will spend more time at the smaller school site, your search will demand more investigation of marginal signals, and your target area will expand outward more.

Also....if the site in question has not been used as a school for a long time the ground may have been filled in or "blown over". By "blown over" I mean the surface of the ground has increased and compacted as the result of winds, storms, changes of seasons, and other natural causes and events. Because of this the coins will be deeper, offer fainter responses, and seem few and far between. Begin your search at this site in the most obvious areas. The playground, the activity area, the lane leading to the school, or path leading to the outhouse (if one is present), and the perimeter of the building itself (front, back and sides). Remember you will be listening for deep coins.... most will be whispers in your headphones.

If the obvious areas do not provide many finds, and let me remind you that the first cursory search of any area is not indicative of what it has to offer, scan the outlying areas. Forget the obvious, and look for the camouflaged or obscure. Remember that open areas may have decreased over time, and expanding your search into the wooded or overgrown "fringe" areas might just produce some excellent finds.

At many of the smaller rural schools I searched over the years I was often fooled by coal (used to heat these old buildings). It sounded off as good, and read high on my detector's meter. If you find this item a problem, check it's metered readout (or if you are using a White's Spectrum XLT...its numerical designation) and cancel it out!

OLD HOMESITES

Old homesites probably offer more potential for decent coin finds than any other site available. The reason of course is the possible discovery of a cache. Caches of money are not found every day, but they are recovered! I am also sure that many of these discoveries are not publicized! What would you do if you dug up as large amount of money?

When searching any homesite always be cognizant of the potential for a cache and proceed accordingly......search every nook and cranny! Oldtimers, homesteaders, colonists, and plain ole, regular folks hid money and the reasons varied. Never mind the purpose...just be alert that this was done routinely years ago, and it's to your advantage to slow down just a little.

Where do you look for a hidden cache? Anywhere and everywhere! Your parameters are determined by the existing condition and accessibility of the site. If the house itself is still standing, and if you are able to search the interior, begin scanning the obvious (although probably not the best) hiding places <u>inside</u> with your sniper coil. Look for loose bricks or stones in hearths or fireplaces. Scan the doors and windows for hollow sills and frames, and of course check the floor boards.

If there's a cellar scan the dirt floor...keeping in mind one or two random coins might turn up in addition to the hoped for cache. Check the steps to the upstairs if the home is two stories, and if the home offers, investigate the appliances that might still be present....stoves, refigerators, sinks, etc....

Remember too that many homes from before the turn of the century had root cellars and storm cellars....potential hiding places

Not enough to retire on, but a nice find in any case!

Consider any place a "hiding" place, and check it out.

for someone's life's savings. As you search continually be thinking ...."if I lived here where would I hide my money?" Where would I put it and feel most comfortable? Would I keep it inside the house so I could reach it quickly, or would I bury it outside somewhere? If I buried it outside would I choose a site that was visible from the house, or would I opt for one out of sight? If I buried it, how deep would I dig? One foot, two feet.... five or six feet? Would it be in an open area or a concealed, camouflaged area? The questions you can ask are endless and the answers will follow suit. The result? You will become more focused on where to concentrate your efforts!

Money caches have been discovered in outbuildings....barns, outhouses and garages. They have been found under fenceposts, near old dumps and under manure. Occasionally under seats in abandoned autos...in rafters of buildings. In tin cans....in old mattresses, in hollow bed posts, in pipes, drainage systems, and in milk cans. In bales of hay, various pieces of farm equipment, and old tree stumps.

Caches might consist of many coins, or just a few. If they are gold it matters not the quantity....what is important is that they are worth face value, and surely a lot more. Seems sacrilegious doesn't it? Thinking like this....all greedy like? Well that's okay, because if you don't get excited over this potential you are not a dye-in-the-wool, coinshooter....! Dreaming about large caches, about instant riches, and searching for them is what it's all about....if you haven't been there you haven't yet begun to enjoy this pastime to it's fullest. Yes you may search a lifetime and never find one, but the fact that they exist, and that you have the equipment and abilities to find them is what it's all about!

Barns, chicken coops, and other types of outbuildings are prime for caches, large and small . . . . search them carefully.

Now that I've gotten you fired up about finding that hidden hoard, what else does an old homesite have to offer? Well it offers the potential for scattered, old coins, and if by chance it has passed through many generations, or families, this potential increases. Where people lived, people relaxed, played, picknicked, worked, entertained, farmed, gardened and homesteaded in general. In doing so they left their mark....or hopefully a few coins.

What makes the old homesite so inviting to the coinshooter is that often it's frequently an unknown entity. It's a site that has been hidden, camouflaged by nature, and overlooked by those that came after. Abandoned, neglected and often demolished...a potentially productive site that just waits for your notice and exploration. They are often difficult to see, because we don't know what to look for, and frequently difficult to search because we don't know what to expect.

Old homesites will always offer the coinshooter the most for his or her time and effort....they are varied, and they are plentiful. You must however understand what "old homesite" means, and more importantly you must know how to find and search them. Finding them is surprisingly easy.....understanding how to work them sometimes is not!

"ONE NICE THING ABOUT GOING HOME IS THAT YOU NEVER HAVE TO MAKE A RESERVATION"

FINDING OLD HOMESITES

How do you find an old homesite? Just where do you begin? Well, it's really not all that difficult! Drive the rural roads in your area. Look for obvious structures, look for clusters of trees in open fields and hidden or concealed lanes that appear to go nowhere. The cluster of trees may have provided shade or beautification for a farmhouse or dwelling. Out of place but with a purpose. The lane or driveway, forgotten and overgrown, leads somewhere...and people had better things to do with their time than to build lanes to nowhere?

Older homesites are also found by comparing old topographical maps with newer ones. Look for indications on the older map...then check to see if they're still present on the new one. If you do not have two topos to compare, drive the area in question, and visually eliminate the structures or okay them for further study. I found map comparisons a lot of fun...almost like doing a crossword puzzle. I wound up with page after page of places to check out, and ultimately lots of old and very productive sites to detect!

> *"Look for clusters of trees in open areas, and overgrown lanes that appear to go nowhere . . . ."*

Older homesites, as might be expected, usually contain a great deal of trash. They were "working" areas....where the people had to toil. As a result it's an area that has an overabundance of iron and steel. Farm implements, parts, nuts and bolts will drive you crazy! What this means is that you will need a great deal more patience. You will also have to allot more time for searching, and you will sometimes have to return again and again to make full use of their treasures. They will inevitably be varied, but they will frequently be valuable....worthy of your ongoing efforts.

When you search an old homesite be sure to check the obvious....the driveway, the path leading to the front door, the backyard, and the most direct paths to any and all outbuildings (if you used them you didn't meander!). Next be sure to cover all the possible hiding places for a cache (which we talked about earlier), and lastly search those areas that are longshots! Outer perimeters, under shrubs, hedges and structures. Incidental coins, over and above the cache, should turn up here and there, and this alone will make your effort worthwhile.

Search all outbuildings....garages, barns, sheds, chicken coops, outhouses and storm cellars. If these structures have dirt floors.....go slow, and dig all reasonable signals. Imagine the routes and intended uses for each structure and search accordingly. Think about how it might have been using the outhouse on a cold day.....just maybe a mad dash provided a few coins in this area?

Old homesites should be searched slowly, and methodically, and if necessary clean out small areas over a period fo time to find the best they have to offer.

Sound silly....maybe? Maybe not! Try being the inhabitant of this home, the homesteader, the farmer, the immigrant, the colonist, the settler, the family man, the father and the provider! What would your life have been like, and how would you have insured a future for your family?

Stone boundary lines are not always abundant with old coins, but can provide one or two keepers . . . . search them!

Let me also mention that many older homesites were surrounded by boundary walls made of rocks. These were built to separate the land from the adjacent owner, and they sometimes can offer an incidental coin or two. They took time to build, and they took manpower. Their construction meant lifting, stooping, standing and other movements which sometimes caused a coin or two to be lost. Not in huges quantities to be sure, but do search these boundary lines when you find them, and dig all of your signals. Trash will not be a problem.....!

Never be in a hurry when searching old homesites.....youmight be surprised and pleased at what turns up. The possibilities are endless, and the odds....not all that bad. Go slow, be ready to dig most of your signals, be patient, and most important, have fun!

Old churches, especially rural ones, can prove to be very profitable . . . .

RURAL CHURCHES

Churches, especially those in the rural areas, are ideal for older coins, but permission <u>must</u> be obtained before you even consider turning your detector on. Churches are private property, and many ministers, priests and churchfolk will not look kindly on you searching their grounds. Permission is not that difficult to get......but do obtain it!

Aside from the immediate outside areas of the church inquire if they had congregational church suppers over the years, and if so, where? These social events, sometimes called harvest home gatherings, were usually held outdoors in a grove area, and not necessarily in the community grove. These church suppers were usually put on two or three times a year, and provided an opportunity for the congregation to get together, eat, play and give thanks. I have searched quite a few such areas, and all surrendered nice coins.

One reason old churches provide good detecting is that those going to church usually had money in their pockets for the collection plate. Some of that, mostly silver, never made it that far.

Scan the path leading from the buggy or auto parking areas to the entrance of the church. Because it's a church site you shouldn't encounter a lot of trash, but be sure to use a probe when hunting well kept areas, and always return any personal items of jewelry that might be found. Doing so will keep you in the minister's good graces as well as that of the Lord!

BEACHES & SWIMMING AREAS

While popular swimming areas will provide you with coins they are not always a favorite of mine. Let me explain.....

Coastal beach areas are fun to detect if your goal is to find a lot of coins, maybe a nice ring or two and get a suntan. Certainly nothing at all wrong with that! I do this often and enjoy it. Know however that any older coins found, especially the silver ones,

My wife Fay hunting the beach in Honolulu, Hawaii . . . .

will probably be corroded from the salt water. If you happen however to be near a shoreline that sometimes gives up a nice coin from an old shipwreck......work it, and work it hard.

One of the best times to search the coastal beaches is immediately after a large storm or hurricane. These severe weather conditions frequently cause a lot of beach errosion, exposing many coins previously out of reach. These storms will also churn up the ocean bottom, allowing coins from areas further out at sea to be washed ashore. You will not be the only one to be hunting these newly available treasures so be ready to roll on a moments notice......it's not at all unusual to find upwards of 50 to 100 detectorists in a beach area when these conditions exist.

Inland swimming sites might be a beach area at a large lake, or merely a bend in the river or creek. Your research and common sense will tell you which offers the best return. There are many older, resort beach areas waiting to be discovered, notated by only a word or two in a local history book. If you are attentive you will reap the rewards. Likewise the proverbial, old swimming hole can also put a few nice coins in your apron.....read, talk to senior citizens, and keep records.

ATHLETIC FIELDS

Athletic fields or stadiums are good only if they are old. They also can look very, very different from one another. Granted baseball is not football, and basketball is not soccer, but I am talking about what might have been the playing fields over one hundred years ago. What did they look like then, and what do they look like today? There's a good possibility they were just large open areas, and still nothing more than that now. Modern stadiums of today are just that.....modern! Totally different from anything that existed decades ago.

Most early sporting events were documented in history books, old newspapers, and school yearbooks. If you are lucky you will also uncover early photos, increasing your odds, and giving you even more to go on. Schools, especially the secondary ones, were often miles apart, and traveling great distances to do battle was not very practical. As a result many such institutions would play each other at a neutral site, often somewhere in-between .... possibly even a farmers field or pasture. Hard to believe today, but a practical reality then.

Old athletic fields, even those from the 30's and 40's can offer many hours of productive searching. The most obvious places to begin....? Under bleachers, on hills overlooking the playing field, entrance or admission area, playing field itself, parking lots, concession or food stands and paths leading to and from any of the above. If the site is still being used you will probably enounter screw caps and pulltabs. My suggestion...set your discrimination to eliminate them, accept the fact that you'll lose a little depth, and go for the silver. If the area has already been hunted heavily......clean out small areas, and then listen for the very deep (and almost always very old) coins others missed!

SCOUT CAMPS

Scout camps are another favorite of mine. Most have been in use for a long time, and with the right approach you can be the beneficiary. I was once given <u>exclusive</u> permission to coinhunt three different scout camps just for giving classes on metal detecting to the scouts. These classes were once or twice a year, but my accessibility to the sites was ongoing. It was a bargain as far as I was concerned, and one camp in particular back in rural New Jersey gave up hundreds of early 19th century silver (not to mention good rings and jewelry).

Most all scout camps have barrack type buildings for those using the facilities, but they also have other areas where tents were pitched, where sports were played, and lakes where happy campers swam, fished and of course lost coins! No secret to finding coins at an area like this, and the best part.....it usually encompassed acres and acres!!

Look for camp listings in your area phone books, and ask local scoutmasters for locations, names and phone numbers, and get to work. Remember again that an offer to share your metal detecting expertise might make the difference in your gaining permission to these areas. Give a little to get a little! I personally enjoyed presenting these classes, and looked forward to being part of their summer programs.

GHOST TOWNS

Each ghost town I've searched over the past twenty two years was different. They pretty much looked nothing like the steriotypical ghost towns of the old west that we read about or imagine. You know what I'm talking about......the weather beaten buildings, the blowing tumbleweeds, the wooden sidewalk and the old corral at the end of town! To be honest the majority of those I hunted gave absolutely no indication whatsoever that they were once a thriving community or town. This will probably be true in your case as well.

No matter where you live you are surrounded by lost and forgotten villages and communities. Make no mistake they are there....not just west of rockies! Communities and towns were abandoned for many reasons. The majority because of lack of earning power. One simply could not contunue to live in an area that did not provide some sort of income, and when the source of the income disappeared, so did the town.

Many of these communities are now hidden by overgrowth, camouflaged and unnoticed by those passing by. A few might offer concrete building foundations for clues, while others offer nothing at all. The buildings themselves could have been removed, bulldozed or burned, and your only clue might be a mention in a history book or newspaper.

*Port Arthur, a ghost town in South Texas, is now nothing more
than scrub and mesquite . . . .*

Your ability to locate such ghost towns depends upon your perserverance, your close scrutiny and of course a little luck. Being the first on the scene can be very exciting and profitable.

THE OTHER AREAS.....

The potential for finding old coins exists most everywhere....where people congregated they lost coins. I covered a few of my favorite sites....now let me touch briefly on a others.

AMUSEMENT PARKS

The older the better, and obviously if still in use obtain written permission. Be prepared for lots of trash, and search the not so obvious for surprises.

SIDEWALK LAWN STRIPS

An often overlooked site that's capable of providing a lot of old coins. This area is public property, and the older the community or neighboorhood the better your chances. Make this a must in your travels.

RURAL CAMPGROUND/REVIVAL MEETING SITES

More prevalent in the south, and always good for old coins. You will probably not be the first to detect them however, so go slow, and listen for the faint, the deep and the valuable.

WINTER SLEDDING AREAS

A favorite of mine, especially when I lived back East. Every town or community had a few spots that offered great sledding. Most still do, and coins lost in snow are very difficult to find. Seek out these areas whenever possible, especially in rural New England towns.

CARNIVAL/CIRCUS SITES

Needless to say these sites attracted large crowds, who in turn lost coins. These attractions were often held in a large field or area in most communities.....perhaps not a big secret but worth checking. A known "money site", but be prepared for lots of trash.....

FRONT YARDS

If you are in an old neighborhood don't hesitate to knock on doors, and ask permission to search front and backyards. Sometimes awkward, but surprisingly easy to get approval for the most part. Return any important jewelry finds to homeowner! These areas are always overlooked because most detectorists are shy.....but remember nothing ventured...nothing gained. You couldn't search the yard before you asked, and if you get turned down, so what....merely status quo!

A COMPREHENSIVE LIST OF POTENTIAL COIN SITES FOR YOUR REVIEW AND CONSIDERATION

1. SCHOOLS
2. PARKS
3. CHURCHES
4. ATHELETIC FIELDS
5. CARNIVAL SITES
6. CIRCUS GROUNDS
7. PICNIC GROVES
8. HOMESITES
9. SWIMMING HOLES
10. SWIMMING BEACHES
11. SCOUT CAMPS
12. GHOST TOWNS
13. PLAYGROUNDS

14. CAMPGROUNDS
15. RODEOS
16. ROADSIDE REST STOPS
17. SIDEWALK GRASSY STRIPS
18. RURAL MAIL BOXES
19. REVIVAL MEETING SITES
20. AMUSEMENT PARKS
21. RURAL DANCE AREAS
22. REUNION AREAS
23. FORT SITES
24. MILITARY INSTALLATIONS
25. WINTER SLEDDING AREAS
26. LOOKOUT/OVERLOOK SITES
27. CHURCH SUPPER GROVES
28. FISHING HOLES
29. RESORTS
30. FISHING CAMPS
31. GENERAL STORES
32. OUTHOUSE AREAS
33. BATTLESITES
34. BAND SHELLS
35. COURTHOUSES
36. RACETRACKS
37. RURAL BOUNDARY WALLS
38. ROADSIDE STANDS
39. COLLEGE CAMPUSES
40. UNDER SEASIDE BOARDWALKS
41. NEAR TELEPHONE BOOTHS
42. AROUND PARKING METERS
43. FLEA MARKETS
44. SKI SLOPES
45. DRIVE IN THEATRES
46. MOTELS
47. VACANT LOTS

48. BUS STOPS
49. OLD TAVERNS
50. OLD INNS
51. CANAL TOWPATHS
52. CONSTRUCTION SITES
53. BARNS & OTHER OUTBUILDINGS
54. FRONT YARDS/BACK YARDS
55. RAILROAD STATIONS
56. FENCE ROWS
57. HIKING TRAILS
58. TRAILER PARKS
59. NEAR HISTORICAL MARKERS
60. OLD GAS STATIONS
61. HIGHWAY CAFES
62. LOVERS LANES
63. TOWN SQUARE

COIN HUNTING OVERSEAS

I will always include a section in any book I write on coin hunting overseas. It is without a doubt the most exciting, the most interesting, and the most profitable coin hunting you will ever do. Finding a coin here from the late 1800's is exciting, but finding one from before the birth of Christ is without equal.

As a result of my involvement with the metal detecting hobby and industry I have traveled overseas to detect with my counterparts in England and France. These experiences were ones that I shall never forget, and as of this date I am looking forward to returning again, and again, and again, and again.

I consider myself very lucky to have so many friends across the seas, and over the past few years I have been invited to spend time in their homes, and to hunt with them in the field. The end result is a sharing, a comraderie and a friendship that will continue forever. Fay and I have also returned the favors, and many of our

Hunting the breathtaking hillsides in Bath, England.

British and French friends have visited us here in Dallas. The problem we always face.....how do we get them excited about a Mercury Dime when they regularly find coins almost 2000 years old? Strangely enough that is not difficult. They are intrigued about out country.....new as it is, and their discoveries of seemingly recent coinage satisfies them......?

I was never much good when it came to American History in High School. It was boring, and one of those subjects that seemed to have no bearing whatsoever on my life then or in the future. Little did I know that I would care a great deal about history later, and little did I know that I would feel lacking when compared to my friends overseas. While I had a hard time remembering what happend 200 years ago their history was over 2000 years old!

I have been fortunate to be able to hunt Roman sites, Celtic sites and areas that could produce coins of extreme value. My finds were many, and while I cannot retire on them, the excitement they provided shall last me the rest of my life, and I am still looking forward to improving on them in the years ahead. The other side of the coin (no pun intended) is that I now have a close kinship to folks across the sea, and this friendship appears to be a lasting one. Spending time with their families in their homes....hunting their sites.....sharing meals, and stories...these are treasures that can never be duplicated or erased, and far more valuable than any coin I will ever find.

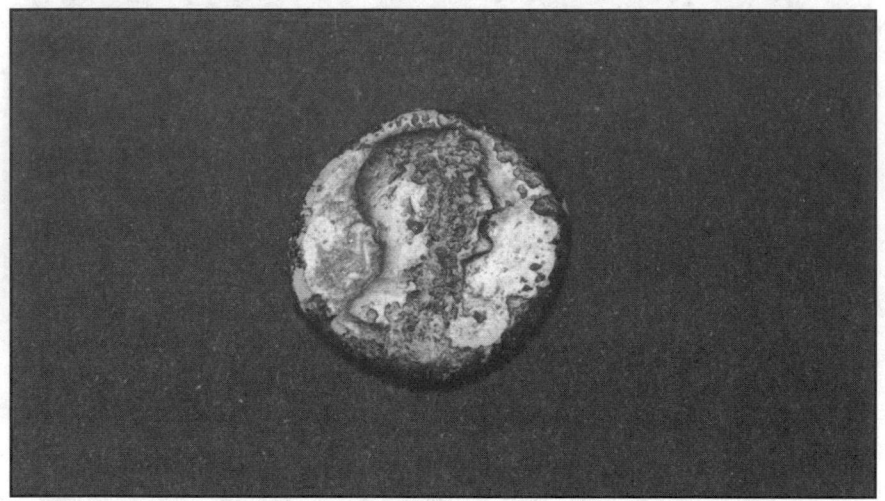

This Roman coin, while not extremely valuable, is one that I shall cherish because of its extreme age . . . .

I will not attempt to tell you about foreign coinage because I am not an authority on this subject. I will state however if you ever have the opportunity to travel to far away places and metal detect.....do it. You won't be sorry!

If you are interested in traveling overseas for some great detecting contact:

DISCOVERY TOURS INTERNATIONAL
3095 Kerner Boulevard "H"
San Rafael, California 94901

A MIXED BAG

Over the past ten years I've written almost 100 articles about metal detecting and coin hunting for the metal detecting magazines. Most of these were for Western & Eastern Treasures, published by People's Publishing Company in Mercer Island, Washington. Some of these articles, because of today's technology are obsolete. Many however stood the test of time, and thanks to Western & Eastern Treasures I've included them in the pages that follow. While some portions of these articles may seem redundant they are worth repeating.....!

FINDING PRODUCTIVE COINSHOOTING SITES
WET, December 1982

Many TH'ers I come in contact with complain about the lack of new and exciting sites to detect, and talk about about the "worked out" schoolyards and parks. They mention their desire to travel, either to find gold out west, relics in the south or gold dubloons on a Florida beach. They're bored to be sure, but I have to laugh because as far as I am concerned new and exciting areas await you just beyond your doorstep.

The reason many of you aren't aware of this is that you are

simply not observant enough, you don't ask the right questions, and you do not follow up the always present clues that abound in your areas. I'm not talking about the old "coinshooting the local schoolyard" routine; I'm talking about coin laden sites that no one has hunted, and are there waiting to be discovered. You're surely asking, "How can I find these areas?" Well, let me back up about two years, and explain just how I became aware of these fantastic sites, and how I continue to find them even now.

About twoyears ago I would have been the first to tell you that finding a decent coin site to detect was becoming difficult, especially if you live in New Jersey, as I do. I continually hit the local schoolyards, the same church grounds, the same parks, and yes I found coins, but finding clad coins no longer interested me. I longed for the prime areas, where no one had ever used a metal detector, and where old and valuable coins were stacked end on end, waiting for me to find them.

Sound too good to be true? Not really! Thanks to an older couple living up the road I did indeed find such an area, and as a result realized that there surely had to be others like it just waiting to be discovered.

The couple I refer to were both retired, and in their mid-sixties. They became close to my wife and I in that they babysat our two children late afternoons until we returned home from work.

They became "family" real quick, and nicer people never lived! In any case they were aware that I spent a great of time metal detecting, and one night mentioned an old "dance area"....just across the road! Had I ever searched there? I looked at them dumbfounded, because across the road was nothing more than a small wooded area. It was triangular in shape, due to the fact that three roads met at that spot, and if I had to guess the area way maybe eighty yards by twenty yards. From all outward appearances it was nothing more than a wooded parcel of land, and gave no indication that it was a site worthy of searching.

DIME A DANCE

They went on to explain that back in the early part of the century, and up to the late forties it was an area used by the locals for Saturday night dances. A large dance floor once stood on the site, as well as two or three refreshment stands, and it was "the place" to be. It was not too uncommon to have two to three hundred people there every Saturday. If you wanted to dance, all you needed to do was pay your way and..... are you ready for the best part.....it was a "dime a dance!" After hearing this I was hoping that no one else knew about this area, and made it a point to get up early the next day to find out.

After arriving at the site I scanned the area, and tried to determine where the dance floor had been. A small concentration of nails on top of ground told me and I began my preliminary search there. I began finding coins almost immediately. Most of them (what else) dimes, and most of them Barber and Mercuries. I found many early dates, and most all were in either fine or extremely fine condition. Mixed in were Indian Head cents, early wheaties, Liberty nickels, and Barber and Standing Liberty quarters. Given that most of the coins were no more than three inches deep it was safe to say I was indeed the first to hunt the site.

For obvious reasons this area became a well kept secret, and was "my" personal close-by honey hole. I continued to detect this area, but after about ten trips the finds began to diminish, and my excitement became lessened. The whole experience had me in a great mood however, and I longed to find another site just like it!

WERE THERE OTHERS?

I began thinking about how this site became available to me, and how often I had passed by it on my way to work, never giving it a second thought. Who would think to detect that small strip of land? I wondered also how many other areas like this escaped my notice. There were certainly others, but to find them I needed help. If I had not been told about the dime a dance site I would have never, ever considered detecting it! I made up my mind then and there to ask everyone I knew for clues to other such sites.

I live in Hunterdon County, a rural county situated in the western central part of New Jersey. Much of the countryside is farmland, most communities small, and founded in the middle 1700's or early 1800's. All I needed to do to find the coins I sought was to find someone about two hundred and eighty five years old! Seriously though the area was rich in tradition and history abounded in the countryside. Having lived in the area for many years I was familiar with many of the local residents, and felt confident that they would help me find other areas like the dime a dance site.

I told everyone I knew and came in contact with about my hobby, and asked them if they knew of any areas that might be worthy of my investigation. This included neighbors, friends, co-workers, and sometimes even strangers. I asked them to ask their friends and relatives, especially the older ones, for ideas.

I would guess that at least 50 percent of those I asked gave me at least one or two promising areas. Old picnic groves came up, areas that were used for sledding in the winter, old swimming holes, ballfields, homesites and so on. The list grew, and I became excited about the possibilities. In some instances the sites mentioned belonged to the people who brought them up....all the better since they were giving me permission to search at the same time! Also many of the people I talked to were curious about my hobby, and later continued to offer clues even after the initial request.

An old picnic grove, that was once the site for old church suppers provided many Indian Head cents, as well a few pieces of silver. A large vacant field, which had once been the only ballpark in the area, also yielded many old and valuable coins. Some sites, as was to be expected, didn't pan out. I can say now however that my batting average is getting better, and the best part is that I still have a list of sites to check out...all potentially rewarding!

MY EYES BEGAN TO OPEN

Being aware of what sites were out there really opened my eyes. Many of them were literally no more than five miles from my front door, yet I had not known about them. Another bonus about areas like this is that you usually aren't bothered by pulltabs or tin foil. Most had been abandoned and forgotten about years and years ago, and were simply waiting for the ambitious and cognizant treasure hunter.

After searching one or two picnic grove areas I quickly became keenly aware of their characteristic traits...low vegetation, plenty of space between large shade trees, and sometimes a stream or creek close by. Add to that an obscure or overgrown lane, and you were on to something worth a try. Because of these clues I knew that a few other wooded sites in my area might have been groves, and I started writing them down for future searches.

Many of my thoughts and hunches panned out, and additional picnic groves were found, as were corner lot ballfields. The ballfields were more often than not hunches only, but given their proximity to small communities and their dimensions I was often right on the mark. My enthusiasm picked up, and my finds increased. I found a new lease on life, and my hobby became exciting once more. All I had to do of course was be aware of what was around me. What really had been there all the time!

I realize I am making all this sound quite easy, and it may not be for all that read this article. Depending upon where you live the clues may not be that predictable or that obvious. Finding such sites might take some time, but if it does it will be time well spent, and the rewards worth the effort.

POTENTIALLY REWARDING SITES

1. FAIRGROUNDS...many are present today, but these sites did not necessarily hold the fairs of long ago. Many times the old areas are nothing more than open fields today, waiting for the coinshooter to turn on his detector!

2. PICNIC GROVES...still look like picnic groves, only no one uses them! Perhaps the old church suppers were held there at one time? Do you know how to define them?

3. SCHOOLS....was the old one room school you discovered always on the present site? It was not unusual at all in the mid 1800's to move one of these small buildings when the landowner decided he needed the land for something else. Research this possibility at the local library!

4. OLD HOME SITES...abound in most all areas. I once found a few that existed deep in the woods simply by talking with a friend of mine who happened to be an avid deer hunter. Many outdoorsmen can provide this type of lead. They often return to the same areas, and know them well. They can also help in obtaining permission to search the sites.

5. OLD BALLFIELDS...are not always apparent to the naked eye. Where did the local ball team play their games before the turn of the century? Could it be that open field just outside of town?

Local history books and school yearbooks can be a big help in finding these productive coinhunting sites.

6. COIN CACHES...not abundant, but how many older folks in your area know of someone who was supposedly very wealthy, and yet died seemingly a pauper? Could it be?

7. SWIMMING HOLES... were as much a part of growing up as was stick ball. Do you know where the kids of your area used to skinny dip? It's a good bet they all went to the same bend in the creek!

8. SLEDDING....has always been a popular sport in the winter, but in order to partake you need a hill. When I was a kid we all went to "Clawson's Hill" and my memories of this area put coins in my pocket. This area shouldn't be hard to find...merely ask any oldtimer.

9. AMUSEMENT PARKS...were much more plentiful in the early part of the century. Your area may not have had one, but I'll bet one wasn't too far away.

10. DANCE AREAS...as mentioned earlier in this article these sites were the place to be on Saturday night. Most were outside, and if you are lucky the one you find will have been a dime a dance as well!

If you are bored and looking for your coinshooting paradise just remember that you don't have to leave home. It's at your doorstep, and yours for the taking!

Dick Stout

GAINING ACCESS TO PRIVATE PROPERTY
WET, March 1984

A question that always bothered me is why so many TH'ers are afraid to ask permission to search private property? Without a doubt there are many, many areas available if only the participants in this hobby would avail themselves of them. Why this does not happen puzzles me! There seems to be an intangible something built into this pastime that, for some reason, we're not proud of, and I think it's time we changed that, as well as our image. Are we embarrassed to be TH'ers? Coinhunters? Relic Hunters? We shouldn't be. We're no different than anyone else who has a hobby. We should be able to participate in it with great enthusiasm and pride.

One way we might start to do this is by being bold, and by taking steps to gain permission to that site we have been looking at for so long. I'm sure we all have such sites, that for one reason or another, we've put off tackling. Usually there is one overriding reason why....the fear of rejection! Sure, asking takes a little nerve, but certainly we can muster up some of that? I hope that in the next few paragraphs I can help some of you with this difficult subject. More importantly, maybe I can inspire a few of you to stand up and take pride in your hobby.

To begin if you have been wanting to detect a certain site, and haven't gotten up your nerve to ask for permission, then stop talking about it and do it. If you don't you'll be thinking about it for years to come, or else you will be hearing about that detectorist who did have the nerve and found coins to put him on easy street. Be frank and ask yourself..."Why am I putting off this task?" I think you'll find that again it's the fear of rejection. To that I say SO WHAT!! You can't detect that site now, so what's the difference if you ask and get a "negative" response? You're status quo....not in any worse shape to be sure. Remember the old saying....nothing ventured...nothing gained!

I consider these requests a 50-50 gamble. Not bad odds at all, especially when you consider the worse that can happen. I'm also willing to bet that, depending on how you approach the owner, you will succeed far more than you fail. Remember again.....nothing ventured...nothing gained.

To start the process approach the owner in one of three ways...in person, via correspondence or via the telephone. Whichever method you decide on prepare for the encounter by putting down on paper exactly what you wish to say, and how you will say it. Realize that you are selling yourself and to do so effectively you must be prepared to sell honesty & integrity just like a salesman. In all likelihood the person you will be confronting will know little, if anything about you or the hobby. The main points you must get across are:

> (1) Who you are, how old you are, where you live, where you work and so on.
> (2) That you are dependable, reputable, courteous and responsible.
> (3) The reason for wanting to search his/her property.
> (4) A brief, but direct explanation of what the pastime is all about.
> (5) That you will detect alone, and not bring friends with you.
> (6) Last but not least, that no matter what his or her answer, you understand the reasons and appreciate their time (if you receive a no initially it might turn into a yes later on).

These may all seem simplistic statements, but certainly ones to consider. To merely talk off the top of your head can often get you into trouble. Write down your thoughts, your approach and in doing so you will succeed far more than you will fail. To be effective you must give the landowner every reason to say yes, and make it increasingly hard for them to say no!

THE LETTER

I personally find that writing to the landowner works best. In a letter you are not having to talk and think on the spot, and you can usually be sure to cover each of the areas I mentioned above in a detailed way. Of course if you are not a great letter writer then you better get out the old books and read up on how to do it.

I have found that letter writing is also less threatening to the landowner, and gives him or her plenty of time to think about your request. Confronting someone at the front door just may kill your chances, especially since we never know the mood he or her will be in. We've all had those "bad" days at one time or another, and confronting the property owner at one of those times does not help your situation. In any case writing helps to alleviate the pressure, and just may make the difference. I have written an example of just such a letter, and hope that you find it of use in your future ventures....

• •

36 Maple Avenue
Smithville, New York 10000

December 1, 1993

Mr. William Jones
123 Main Street
Jonesboro, New York 10000

Dear Mr Jones:

Please allow me to introduce myself. My name is James

Johnson. I'm 35 years old and I have lived in Jonesboro well over six years. I work as a mechanic at Wheaton's service station, and I am married, with a teenage daughter.

In my sparetime I enjoy the hobby of metal detecting, and I am always looking for new and different places to detect. Just recently it was brought to my attention that your vacant lot used to be the site of many atheletic events in the past, and I am hoping that you might allow me search it at sometime in the future.

I have been metal detecting for over ten years now, and find it a healthful and enjoyable pastime. The fun of finding old an interesting items such as coins, jewelry, buttons, pen knives, etc. never fades. I always respect the property that I'm allowed to search, and always leave it exactly as it was upon my arrival. I do no noticeable digging (a small probe and/or trowel is all that I employ) and assume all liability for any accidents that may occur while on that property. I also promise to abide by any restrictions or stipulations you may make with regards to accessiblity to the area in question, and promise to never bring anyone else with me.

I realize that this is a rather unusual request, especially since you do not know me personally. I can, if you so desire, supply you with a number of references, both personal and business. I would obviously prefer the direct approach in meeting you, but also feel that a letter such as this often works better than a knock on your door. I have enclosed a self addressed, stamped envelope in case you wish to reply in the same manner, but if I do not hear from you within a week or two I will stop by your residence to introduce myself.

I will certainly understand if you refuse this request. Whatever your decision please know that I appreciate your time and trouble. Thank you very much....

Sincerely,

James Johnson
Phone (807) 377-1234

Whenever you approach any landowner try to put yourself in their place. How would YOU feel if you were suddenly approached by a complete stranger, requesting permission to look around YOUR property? By reversing the roles you tend to get a better idea of just what to expect during this confrontation. Each site, or for that matter, each owner, may dictate an entirely different approach, and it's up to you to find out which is best at the time. Not an easy chore to say the least. Whatever you decide to do, and however you decide to do it, have a positive attitude. It can only help, and always remember that you only get once chance to make a first impression. Remember also that you are selling yourself, as well as the hobby, and how you handle yourself will reflect on all of us.

Be proud to be a treasure hunter...a coinshooter. If all you ever do is a little coin hunting, for a few hours a week, you're still a treasure hunter...a metal detector user. Enjoy your hobby...do it with fervor and enjoy every minute of it. Don't lose that positive attitude. Be bold and be assertive. You've been dreaming about running your detector over that site for some time now, and wishing isn't going to make it happen. Believe me, there are many new sites to detect, and many new treasures to be found. I intend to work at finding them. How about you?

THE NOT SO OBVIOUS HOTSPOT
WET, May 1983

Virtually all coinshooters have searched, at one time or another, what I would call the typical site. By typical I mean the local park, the local school, the local church and so on. Fairly common territory for most of us, and the reasons are obvious as well. They are close, they seldom fail to produce a few finds, and one feels comfortable in familiar territory.

Searching such sites is fine, but I would like to pass on a few ideas of mine and delve into the "not so obvious" potential hot spots within each area. These are suggestions and only that. They are not meant to be fool-proof. They are reflections based upon many years of coinshooting, as well as detailed record keeping. Hopefully by sharing them with you, you may be able to increase your finds in the future.

FOOTBALL FIELDS

Most all football games attract fairly large crowds, and one can usually expect to find coins at such an area. The playing field itself, and the grandstand area are the first and most obvious places to search, but after trying your luck there, give the following a try....

Wherever there are crowds there must be a place for one to park a car. Most of these parking areas are usually adjacent to the playing area, and at some rural schools are merely fields.

Reaching into one's pocket for car keys, or the cost of admission can result in lost change, and I have found this area to be quite profitable.

The next area to search would be the entrance. Here larger denominations of coins (dimes, quarters and halves) were handled and frequently were dropped and lost. While most fields today have ticket booths/buildings for this purpose it was not unusual in the past to have people standing at the entrance taking money and handing out tickets. Search the perimeter of a football field as well, and you may be able to locate this particular spot. Keep in mind that it may very well be located somewhere other than where the entrance is now.

Another good hot spot is directly behind the grandstand area. Note I said "behind" the grandstand area. Yes, under the grandstand is good, but so is the junk that you will encounter, and getting to this area is not an easy task. I personally have more luck to the rear of the stands. The next time you attend a high school football game observe what goes on in this area, and perhaps you will understand why it's a good one to detect. Bored children, who would rather do anything other than watch a football game, often start their own game in this area, and more often than not spend much of their time on the ground.

Many spectators, imprisoned in their upper grandstand seats, usually have someone else do their refreshment buying for them. That someone will usually receive their money by catching it while standing at the rear of the grandstands. Not an easy chore for the most part, and keep in mind not too many people will throw pennies.

CHURCHES

If you like to detect old churches in your area let me share some ideas with you relative to my experiences in this type of site. Please note I said "old" churches...not new. You can search newer structures if you wish, but don't expect to find older coins, because you can't find them where they AIN'T!

The first tendency in hunting such an area is to hunt the main entrance or path leading to the entrance. This of course makes sense, but don't foreget that people had to park something, whether a car or a buggy, in order to even arrive at the church. This area, if not known, can't be too far away from the front door of the church and a little perseverance on your part could very well find it.

Another favorite of mine is the closest grove area to the church, and in many cases it is adjacent or in back of the building. Many churches used to have harvest home suppers, which were the highlight of the year for the parishoners, and usually attracted many. They were held in the closest picnic area, and if one looks closely he can sometimes determine where that was. Most grove areas I have searched are usually dominated by very large trees, and very low ground vegetation. The distance separating the trees is quite large, which of course allowed for eating areas and outdoor activity.

BASEBALL FIELDS

While the local Baseball field may be located in close proximity to the school or football field, it nonetheless has a few characteristics that set it off from the other areas. Again the obvious hotspots are the spectator areas, the homeplate area and around the bases. They are productive to be sure, but here's two more to consider.

Assuming you are a baseball enthusiast or fan try the "gaps" in the outfield (left-center, right center), as well as close to each foul line. My reason for suggesting these areas may not "hold water" with too many detectorists, but I feel that outfielders tend to dive after balls not hit directly at them, and in doing so loose more change in these areas? What do you think? Whatever your answer I can assure you that my experience has proven these areas better for coins than the the most obvious? Give them a try and see how you do?

The next area to detect...down the foul lines, in foul territory. Many people shun the seated areas, and prefer to lay on blankets or the grass itself. A couple of lovers, someone with a small child, but again whatever the reasons this is usually a good site to search.

SCHOOLYARDS

With the increasing popularity of metal detectors, forget the playground area. It's hunted to death, and at most will only give up a few clad coins. If the school dates back some, start your search at the very perimeter of the mowed area. One usually tends to shy away from this area, and it usually produces many decent finds.

My theory is that perhaps the activity area was larger in the past, and due to the amount of time spent keeping it in shape or due to the laziness of the many caretakers, it has diminished in size. Again an assumption, but accurate record keeping has proved to me that it is indeed a hot spot in most every instance.

Next search any hills or slopes that may be present in the school area. They were, and are still used by many youngsters for eating lunches, playing games, watching other activities or simply for soaking up some sun. Check the entire hill, both top and bottom, as well as the slope itself. Most older coins will not be that deep, due to the terrain and natural errosion.

PARKS

Most any area of a park can produce coins, but if your local park is located in the center of town try the perimeters again. It's where people arrive at the site, where they park their cars, and where they attempt to carry their belongings into the area.

If there is an area for picnicking choose an area approximately ten yards by ten yards, and literally clean it out. Retrieve whatever trash is present, and repeat the same process again and again. Not a novel idea to be sure, and certainly a lot of work. Because it is so consuming those coins you do find will usually be keepers and worth the effort.

Lastly search the open areas within the park. They afford many the opportunity to participate in vigorous activities, and a real good chance at losing money and valuables.

If your time is limited, and you do indeed hunt these routine sites do not feel bad about it. I'm positive that they still offer good finds, but you must change your thinking and you in the process hit those areas that seem less likely to produce. I am certainly not guaranteeing you instant riches....but I am somewhat confident that you will be pleasantly surprised!

RESEARCHING YOUR LOCALE
WET, July 1983

The dictionary defines the word "research" as "diligent, protracted investigation". A truer definition for the treasure hunter never existed, or should I say successful treasure hunter. How valuable, how old, and how consistent your finds are depends largely on how diligently you research. "Every now and then" research usually results in "hit or miss" finds. Any treasure hunter, no matter how inexperienced, can increase his chances by knowing what to look for and where to look for it.

The first and most obvious place to start researching your local area is at libraries. Note that I said libraries, not library. It is important to realize that there are many libraries available to every TH'er, and to not check them all out could mean being the last one to a new and very productive site. There are, without doubt, many libraries within easy driving distance of your home, and in all likelihood all will have information available on your locale.

Do not for an instant think that just because you've exhausted the local library's area history section that you are through, or that there is nothing more to be learned. Make sure you hit them all. A different book, a different author, written from a different perspective, or from different sources, could be just what you're after!

BOOKS TO LOOK FOR

Books to look for would include your town or township, county and state histories. (Keep in mind that this is just your starting point, and that there are many other towns and townships within easy reach of your doorstep). These books will usually include information regarding the first schools, churches, railroads, parks and outdoor events in the area. All very useful information for the coinshooter, however you must remember to read very carefully and take accurate notes.

For instance the first school built in your town or township is important information since it may be potential site, but you must also note how long this particular school was in existence, and where it was located. If it was in use for only a very short period, which was quite common years ago, you might find that further research will not be worth the time.

It was not at all unusual in years past for small one room schools to come and go or to be moved for that matter. They were literally picked up and moved in those days, and it could be that you will be wasting your time searching around it when in fact it may have stood at another site for a much longer period? Finding that spot would certainly offer you a better return on your time.

Local history books will frequently refer to turn of the century sites in generalities. Areas were often named after the landowner at the time, but later renamed to accomodate the many changes that took place in the community. You might find a passage that reads "this rural, one room school was situated on the Jacob Reed property, north of Everitt's Hill road". To begin with Everitt's Hill road is, in all likelihood, now called something else, possibly even a numbered highway. Secondly Jacob Reed has long since passed on, and the property probably has changed hands many times. Also if Everitt's Hill road is ten miles long where is north of it? Sound silly....it's not! I continually found such vague information, but remember that when it was written or recorded it was not so vague.

Most all libraries will have old maps for your reference, and hopefully a few from different time frames or eras. Look for the earliest maps of the area you can find and study them intensely. If possible make copies of them. Remember that very early maps (or plates as they were called) were not as detailed or as accurately drawn as those of today. Most land areas again were named for the landowner, and finding the same location on a new map may take some doing. Try to always work your way forward from older maps, going from the very oldest to next oldest, and on up to the latest.

Hopefully this overlay or transformation will make some sense, and offer you a good place to start your search.

With any luck you will come up with the exact site or location you seek. A check of the county tax records will then give you the name and address of the current owner, and with any luck the permission you need to bring home the rewards of your hard work.

Other useful sources are the local town centennial or bi-centennial publications. They are most always filled with very useful information, and typically carry more photos than does a history book. An event such as a centennial is usually a "big deal" for a small town, and offers it's citizens a reason to celebrate and have fun. Because of this these publications are put together with "lighter" types of information, and often center around the older carnivals, the local baseball teams, the older picnic areas, the old swimming holes and so on. They will often include many reflections or "fond looks back" as offered by many of the area's older folk.

This type of information is just what the coinshooter ordered, and the photos can be extremely useful for pinpointing exact locations and hot spots, such as the refreshment stand location at the local athletic field, the bath house site at the beach, etc..

FAMOUS TOWNFOLK

Perhaps your area had a few famous inhabitants years ago. Perhaps they were rich and famous. Perhaps there are legends or tales concerning their lives, or more important their riches? Know who they were, and read about them. Many times legends or old tales are nothing more than rumors passed down through the years....however if enough books or enough sources make mention of them you must take notes. You never know where your next lead will come from, and if nothing else you will probably find it interesting reading, and in the process know and appreciate your community more.

An interesting sidelight.... You will automatically start getting interested in your local history from a learning perspective. Believe me it will happen whether or not you intend for it to. You will become intrigued and fascinated with the many, many documents, facts and figures you turn up, and inadvertenly you will become somewhat of a local historical buff!

Keep in mind that research at the libraries is only one very small facet of your overall plan. Don't forget to join your local historical society, and don't forget to spend some time looking through your local newspaper's microfilm files. Both can add new information to your files as well as help you to build on previously started leads. Don't forget to check out all of your neighboring towns and townships as well. Be meticulous in your reading and your note taking since your sources will vary (and quite possible a few of the facts you uncover). Be aware of any footnotes listed in history books and bibliographies. They can offer additional information on the subject in question if needed. Look for obvious words: Schools, churches, parks, railroads, picnic areas, amusement parks, swimming areas, carnivals, outdoor dance sites, athletic events, revival meetings, lovers lanes, scout camps, hotel sites, stagecoach stops, old groves and so on. Anything that might offer you a reasonable return on your time and effort....!

Trying to cover the entire topic of research is not possible in the space alotted me here, but I do firmly believe the key to being a successful coinshooter is in being a persistent and dedicated researcher. Read, read and read some more. Follow up every lead where possible. Some will turn sour on you, others may produce, but remember the definition of research. If you are diligent in your efforts sooner or later you will hit paydirt!!

CONCLUSION

I hope that you've enjoyed reading *Coin Hunting… In Depth!* I had fun writing it, and hope that in doing so I was able to make you a better coin hunter.   Ultimately the success you have will be the direct result of the time and effort you put in.   Persistence, perserverance and accurate research are also major ingredients in the recipe. Mix them with good equipment, a little intuition, a lot of common sense and you can't miss!

No matter how many coins you find, and no matter how rich you might become, the best part of coin hunting is the hunt itself! The wonderment of what you might unearth, and the thrill of discovery is very real, and as such makes this pastime one of the most exciting in the world today.   I am richer in many ways as a result of participating, and feel certain you will be too!

Good hunting, and who knows….. maybe I'll see you in the field one day!

Dick Stout

NOTES

Dick Stout

NOTES

NOTES

NOTES